NOBODY CARES... WORK HARDER

STEVE WILMER

Apex Media & Publishing LLC
6847 N. 9th Ave Ste A336
Pensacola, Fl 32504
www.ApexMediaPublishing.com

Ordering Information:
Quantity Sales. Special discounts are available on quantity purchases by corporations associations, and others. For details contact the publisher at the address above.

ISBN-13: 978-1981948369

ISBN-10: 1981948368

Published by Apex Media & Publishing LLC
Written by Stephen C. Wilmer & Erin L.Wilmer
Edited By Ervin Byrd
Cover Design by Eldric Connors
Interior Design by Elden Scott

Published in the United States of America

CONTENTS

NOBODY CARES... WORK HARDER

INTRODUCTION

STEVE WILMER

NOBODY CARES... WORK HARDER

INTRODUCTION

I was on a plane headed to speak in Bakersfield, California. While most watch a movie, listen to music or sleep, I always read first. I reached into my bag and pulled out a book given to me by my friend Scott Heyka. The name of the book is *The Miracle Morning* by Hal Elrod. I began to read about Hal's journey from where he began to what propelled him to where he is now. In short, he'd had a successful life, or what most would consider a successful life, because unfortunately most of us don't live life, we simply exist in life. But Hal wanted more. He wrote, "I worked 365 days straight, selling and writing, with a level of discipline which eluded me the first 25 years of my life. I was fueled by passion to do what I had never done before: To venture from my painfully comfortable realm of mediocrity – from which I operated my entire life – into the space of being extraordinary." I nearly jumped out of my seat when I read this. It provoked me, but simultaneously it was also a punch to the gut, because I know that I have been living in a painfully comfortable realm of mediocrity. Most people do.

In the movie Braveheart, William Wallace, played by actor Mel Gibson, uttered a profound statement

"Every man dies, not every man truly lives." Is that you? Are you merely existing and not living your life to the fullest? Are you experiencing everything that your Creator has for you? We take great pleasure in boasting that we are a survivor when we should be thriving; having more, doing more and giving more.

I attended a magnificent event in Las Vegas a while back called "Go Pro". It was an event for the Network Marketing profession. There were over 20,000 entrepreneurs in attendance, those who live life according to what they want, and not according to what someone else wants to give them. Over a three-day period we listened to dozens of millionaires and a few billionaires, like Virgin Atlantic Group Founder Sir Richard Branson, discuss with us entrepreneurship. From the stage, Go-Pro Founder Eric Worre shared with us how he was excited to tell his friend Tony Robbins, also in attendance, how he'd grown his Go-Pro business tremendously; how he was making moves that he'd never made before and experiencing a success he's never had before. Tony's reply, "You're playing small." Ouch! Basically, Tony was telling Eric that he had more on the inside of him. Eric had more to do and more to give.

On a side note, you should definitely get yourself

to a Tony Robbins event. My wife and I attended a UPW (Unleash the Power Within) event and it took us to the next level in every area of our lives. We all need that someone in our life who doesn't drink the Kool-Aide; Someone who doesn't tell us what we want to hear, but tells us rather what we need to hear. We need that person who will challenge us along our journey. My favorite book of the Bible is James. James told it like it was and made no apologies. We all need a "James" in our life. God has blessed me over the years that whenever I finish speaking I am showered with congratulations, applause and adoration. Now I would be lying if I said that it didn't feel amazing to receive such accolades, but hearing, "You did well" all the time doesn't help us, it hurts us. Good job, all the time doesn't make us grow. If it doesn't challenge us, it won't change us. We won't become better. The "yes" grows our bank account but the "no" grows us. We've all heard the term, "Whatever doesn't kill you makes you stronger." I absolutely agree with that. But most of us don't want to experience the pain to receive the results. No pain…No gain.

When I went to visit my good friend Andi Duli, one of those millionaires from the Go-Pro event, at his home in Oklahoma, I began telling him about the success of my speaking career, book sales and marriage. I remarked that I was now enjoying a six-figure income and life was good. His reply was a punch in the gut. He simply asked, "Just good? Not great? God want's great for your life." Although I was experiencing success that I'd never experienced before, I was still living in a painfully comfortable realm of mediocrity. But that remark also help set me on a journey to becoming a better person and a better entrepreneur. It challenged me to start thinking differently about the so-called success that I was experiencing.

One of my favorite messages from Pastor Joel Osteen is entitled, "Don't Settle for Good Enough." All these events have led me to realize that I too am playing small. There is more on the inside of me to give, so that's the reason for this third book. My first book 10 to Win was good. Actually, I can't stand to read it anymore because I've changed (grown) so much in the two years since I've written it, I'm not sure that I agree with everything in it anymore. It's lacking. My second book, Supercharge Your Multi-line Agency was co-authored with my good friend, author and speaker, Bill Whitley. It is an absolute must for any insurance professional. We share proven techniques for closing more sales & building the agency of your dreams. While I am extremely proud of both of these accomplishments, I was playing small. I was holding back.

Nobody Cares, Work Harder (NCWH) is an "in your face, no holds barred, put up or shut up" type book. Some of you may be offended and that's okay. I didn't write this book so that you will like me. I wrote it so that it can help change your life for the better. Sometimes offense is the only thing that will spark us to get off of our butt and do something about it. As a matter of fact, too many things today offend us. We get distracted with offenses and we take our eyes off the ball, causing us to once again simply survive rather than thrive. Do you ever notice how it's only the broke people (people living from paycheck to paycheck) who are offended? Rich people don't have time to get offended. Rich people are too busy making moves, on a mission to change their lives to be worried about what the media is saying or who offended them. So, if you're offended over everything then maybe you don't have enough going on in your life. I believe I just said, "If you're offended, get a life." *NCWH* will also challenge you. Some things will hurt. It will force you to take an honest look at your life. It did for me as well. I'm writing this book not from a place of success like I have it all together, but to share my honest journey with you. And maybe together we can hold each other accountable to have that exceptional life we've all daydreamed about. I haven't arrived... but I've left.

There are a few people who I would like to acknowledge.

I want to thank my family, who without their continued support none of this would be possible. To my four well-mannered children Judah, Josiah, Joi and Jayna, I love you all so much. Thanks for loving me even when I am at times un-lovable. You know better than anyone that dad is not always motivational at home. To my lovely wife of 20yrs, thank-you Erin for holding down the fort when I'm traveling, living my purpose, walking in my calling. You are my biggest fan and supporter. Please keep being the "James" in my life although it doesn't feel good at that moment. Thank you for your work on *NCWH*. I appreciate you so much. 143

As Forrest Gump proclaimed, "I am not a smart man." But I am smart enough to surround myself with people who are smarter than I. I get all the glory, while they do all the work behind the scenes. Thank you to Lance Cook for your amazing work on all my social media success. You Rock my friend. Thank you to

Eldric Connors for your remarkable work on my first audio CD "Inspired.", and my website. You took it to the next level. Get ready, I was playing small on that one. Thank you to Ervin Byrd for your ideas and edits on all of my book projects. I appreciate you my friend. And of course, thank you Elden Scott for remaining on this journey with me. Your work on *10 to Win* and now *NCWH* has been nothing short of marvelous.

Lastly, I want to go on record as thanking the Holy Spirit. It was he that gave this book to me. I pray that I follow his lead as I write upon these pages. I pray that many lives will be changed for the better. Have your way Holy Spirit.

When New York Times best-selling author and speaker Dr. John C. Maxwell is about to deliver a hard dose of reality to his audience, he warns, "My name is John, and I'm your friend" in order to soften the blow. As you read Nobody Cares, Work Harder …remember, "My name is Steve and I'm your friend."

NOBODY CARES... WORK HARDER

I DON'T WANT TO HEAR IT!

CHAPTER ONE

NOBODY CARES... WORK HARDER

I DON'T WANT TO HEAR IT!

It's 4am Sunday morning. I'm lying awake in bed and for some reason I can't sleep. My mind starts to wander about my upcoming Las Vegas event. I'm excited and nervous at the same time. I start thinking about the kids about to go back to school and a whole laundry list of other things on my mind. Parenthetically, my thoughts travel at 100 miles an hour. Anyone else have that problem?

My thoughts shift to my good friend Ervin Byrd, Jr., the editor of *NCWH.* Ervin's father, Ervin Byrd, Sr., aka Papa Byrd, recently passed away. Ervin and his father were extremely close and his death understandably shook Ervin. We were on the phone talking and I asked Ervin where was he calling from? He told me he'd just gotten off work from his overtime shift. "Work?", I replied. But your father recently passed. Ervin's response was classic. "Yes work! The bills are still due. The mortgage company doesn't care that I lost my father. They want their money. The power company doesn't care that I lost my father; they want their payment. The grocery store doesn't care that I lost my father; they want money, if I want to continue to feed my family. My job doesn't really care that I lost my father, either. They gave me a few days off but if I want more days off it will be without pay. They are not going to give me money if I don't work." People always say, "Let me know if there's anything I can do to help. But in short, they are not going to pay my bills. I must pay them. So yes, I am at work."

I jump out of bed and go to my laptop because I must put this in *NCWH*. Ervin gets it. Ervin understands. You didn't have enough time to finish the job? Nobody cares, work harder. You're short staffed at work? Nobody cares, work harder. Not feeling well today? Nobody cares, work harder. Tried your best but still can't get the job done? Nobody cares, work harder. Your father just passed away? Sadly, nobody cares, work harder. Now, for those of you thinking that Ervin should be given a pass because of his father's death, you my friend are an excuse maker. Most of us believe that people should be given a pass because of their circumstances. And with that belief we will never reach our highest potential in life. I would gather to say that with this mindset, if we look back over our life we have made excuse after excuse. It's most likely the reason that we're not living the life of our dreams at this very moment.

Until we start to take responsibility for our actions or our non-actions, we will remain in the same place we are now, which is most likely living broke and broken; living from paycheck to paycheck at a dead-end job that we hate, or we simply tolerate. We stay there because we've made excuses about why we can't move on.

I was there. I was broken and broke. I was broken because of my circumstances growing up in the projects on welfare. I won't go into that because there is no need. We can all imagine the life of a little child in the projects. The media has done a wonderful job of showing us that. I won't use that an excuse to fail in life. We are not a product of our circumstances: We are a product of our decisions. Oh, I'm so sorry that you grew up on welfare. Whatever, nobody cares, work harder. Your father wasn't around to mentor you as a child? Nobody cares, work harder. You found out years later that the man you thought was your father turned out not to be him at all? Crushing, but nobody cares, work harder. Life continues to go on. We must stop making excuses about why we can't succeed. I'm not saying that it's going to be easy. There are some real-life things that happen to all of us. Some of these things make it more difficult for us to succeed. Some circumstances make it extremely difficult to succeed. Again, I say difficult but not impossible. Remember that life is only 10% of what happens to us and 90% of how we respond to it. But succeed we must. I have a hand written note on my bathroom mirror that reads, "Success and Nothing Less." We can't let the circumstance win. We must dig our heels in, put our heads down, grind like we've never grinded before and keep moving forward. Don't stop, don't quit. I'm not saying that it's going to be easy, I'm saying that it's going to be worth it. Once you achieve your dreams, you will look back and discover that all the hard work paid off. Remember, nothing that lasts will come easy. And nothing that comes easy will last. Yes, I understand that I don't know what you may be going through, but the hard truth is this, nobody cares, work harder.

It wasn't until I became a United States Marine that I started to have the confidence I needed to succeed. Before I forget, if you're struggling with confidence, join the Marine Corps Infantry. You'll never have that issue again. How about this, when I was in boot camp my drill instructor didn't care about my background. He didn't care that I didn't have a daddy. He didn't care that I was poor, black, stupid, or scared. I had a job to do and he expected me to do it. He essentially expected me to excel at it. If I wanted to be able to call myself a US Marine I had better get the job done. He didn't except any excuses from me. Those who gave excuses found themselves on a bus ride home or in the Navy. Sorry I couldn't help myself. My wife is a retired Navy Chief Petty Officer and this is what we do, poke fun at each other in love. For those keeping score. Marines 1, Navy 0. Now, where was I? Oh yea, because my drill instructor didn't accept any excuses, and I mean NO EXCUSES at all. It required me to push myself. It required me to go above and beyond. I began to do things that I had no idea that I could do. There were plenty of occasions where I wanted to give up. But he didn't accept excuses so I didn't. There were times when I wanted to quit but he didn't allow it so I didn't. There were times when the task was unbearable and I reverently believed that it couldn't be done. But he didn't accept any excuses so guess what? I got the job done. That's why it's so important to have those people around us to push us when we want to quit; those who won't accept our excuses.

Listen to me. When I lost all of my excuses, I found all of my results. My excuses were keeping me at a good job where I was experiencing good success, so I thought. Remember Hal's story from the beginning of the book? I was a star employee in the insurance industry. I wanted more, but my excuses kept me bound. Fear (an excuse) kept me bound. The only thing standing between us and our goal is the story we keep telling ourselves as to why we can't achieve it. What's your story? When I stepped out on faith (and God's promises) I excelled. What did I just say? When I lost all of my excuses, I found all of my results. I've never been happier at any career as I am now. I am living my passion. Someone once said that when you love what you do, you'll never work a day in your life. Writing this book is not work. Speaking and encouraging audiences is not work. Training agents and their team on the phone is not work. All these things fulfill me, and quite honestly, they are extremely easy for me to do because it's my passion. The challenge for me is to keep taking it up a notch and to never settle for where I am, and the moderate success that I am having.

The problem is that we've been taught from a young age that excuses are okay if they're good enough. So rather than becoming good at our trade or our job, we've adapted to becoming good at making excuses. Excuses have been around since the beginning of creation. In the Garden of Eden, God told Adam and Eve not to eat of the forbidden fruit. When God questioned Adam about his disobedience, rather than taking responsibility, he blamed it on Eve. When God questioned Eve about it, she blamed it on the serpent. It started for most of us in elementary school when the teacher gave us a homework assignment. If we didn't complete the assignment she would ask, "Why didn't you do your homework?" I was a terrible student in school so I learned pretty quickly that if my excuse was good enough I would get a pass. Sometimes it worked and sometimes it didn't. Rather than holding me accountable for not doing the work, I received extra time. This taught me that deadlines really weren't that important. That bad habit continued throughout my years in school; Give a good enough excuse, get a pass. Society has taken that same mentally and magnified it. We see it in the workplace, on television, in our government and in the home. Excuses are everywhere. Everyday we hear, "I didn't get the job done because _____________."

I currently train over 150 agents and team members on a monthly basis. During the training sessions, I often give the team members assignments to complete by a certain day. They must make a certain amount of sales or speak with a certain number of people. Their goals have been set. When the deadline approaches I go around the room and ask, "Did you hit your goal? The ones who missed their goal invariably say, "No because I __________________." They always have an excuse. They never simply say no I didn't hit my goal. So now when they start to give their excuse (or reason-call it what you wish) I say, "Listen, I have a tiny little box to write YES or NO. The box is only big enough for one word. I don't have room for an excuse. They become almost offended, "It's not an excuse, it's real." I remain firm that my box is only big enough for one word. They are now upset with me, because I refuse to accept their inability to get the job done; As if it's my fault they missed their mark. The nerve of me to hold them accountable. But that's the world we live in. Are you one of those people who believe that the world should give you a pass if you miss the mark because your excuse or your reason is good enough? And why do we hate the word excuse? It is what it is. We are offended (all of us) if someone says, "You're making excuses." It's almost like they're calling us a liar to our face. Or perhaps we feel like they don't believe us; that maybe we're trying to pull the wool over their eyes.

So, lets take a quick minute and take a look at the definition of excuse. Excuse: An attempt to lessen the blame; seek to defend or justify; a reason or explanation put forward to defend or justify a fault. When we give excuses, this is exactly what we're doing, like it or not. The definition of reason reads pretty much the same; To give an explanation or justification for an action or event. Once again, I am justified for failing to complete the task because ____________________. There's an old saying, "Excuses are like armpits. Everyone has them and they all stink." Of course that's the PG version. None of us want to hear excuses, we all want results. Remember that the next time you are about to give your justification about why you didn't get the job done…and don't!

I am not exempt from excuses either. It's so engrained in our DNA. At times, I must catch myself. My good friend Kari Dunham was spearheading a fundraiser, collecting gift cards for our kids school, Trinitas Christian. She asked me to obtain a number of gift cards by a certain day and I agreed. When the deadline came I did not have all of them. Before I knew it, I was making excuses, "I've been extremely busy with travel, I'm preparing for my event in Vegas, I'm writing my 3rd book", all which were true. But it didn't negate the fact that I did not complete the task in the time allotted. I cut out the excuses, asked for forgiveness and told her that I would have them all the following week… and I did. By the way, Kari is a Navy pilot, so she wasn't accepting any excuses that I offered. I think there is a trend here. Perhaps everyone should spend some time in the military. It would cut out a lot of issues we have in our society, and that's just my two cents.

Winston Churchill was the former British Prime Minister during WWII. The story goes that his generals were losing battle after battle. He brought his generals in and asked what seemed to be the problem? They began giving excuses (imagine that) and proclaimed, "We're doing our best." Churchill's response was classic. He remarked, "I don't need you to do your best. I need you to do what's necessary." Ouch! How many of us say those words? I'm doing my best. Once again, we offer the excuse to justify our failure. We then feel good because we've been taught all our lives to do our best. And if we're doing our best what else can we do right? Wrong! Our best may not be good enough. Our best may actually suck. If our best is not getting the job done then maybe we should look for a new job or a whole new career. Maybe this is not for us. Maybe we should go do something that requires no real skills, that's not too hard, no pressure and is pretty easy to do. I mean if we're doing our best then we have nothing else to give, right? I would submit that most of us aren't really doing our best. I would definitely submit that most of us aren't doing what's necessary.

How much time do we spend practicing our craft? What personal development have we done? Who have we asked for help? Have we taken their advice? Have we picked up a book? Have we studied it back and forth? Have we practiced on our own time? My good friend Mitchell Price is a former NFL player. He said that they would run drills and practice over and over, not until they got it right, but until they couldn't get it wrong. Are you willing to put that kind of work into it? Or are you good with your excuses?

There are a few people that I follow on Facebook and YouTube for my motivation, inspiration and information. Among these individuals is four-time Best Selling Author and speaker Gary Vaynerchuk. His methods are not for everyone. If you like things to be candy-coated then Gary is not for you. But if you're like me (rip the band-aid off) then Gary is your man. His style and language is colorful, clear and straight to the point. In one of his talks he was addressing a room full of entrepreneurs and one of them began to complain about the laws in the state which prevented him from pursuing a new business. Gary quickly cut him off and told him (PG version) "Nobody cares about your feelings. Nobody owes you anything. People cry about the way they want things to be instead of reacting to the way it actually is." Excuses! It's too hard, the rates are too high, the competition is cheaper, I tried my best, waaahhh! Get over it. I don't want to hear it.

Jim Rohn remarked, "Don't wish it were easier; wish you were better." Become better and stop with all the crying and excuses. Yes, it's hard. If it were easy then everyone would do it. Once again, I'm not telling you it's going to be easy, I'm telling you it's going to be worth it. Nothing that lasts comes easy, and nothing that comes easy will last, remember?

When I was in the insurance industry, I kept a sign on my desk for my customers to see. It sat right in front of them so they couldn't help but see it. Anytime they began to tell me why they couldn't purchase the product, I would ask them to read my sign out loud. The sign simply read, "If it's important to you, you will find a way. If not, you will find an excuse." So, the bottom line for most of us is that if the task at hand, the goal is truly not a priority for us. It's not important to complete the task. So once again we make an excuse to justify our actions, or should I say lack of action. Founding Father Benjamin Franklin remarked, "He that is good at making excuses is seldom good for anything else."

Ouch again! What are you good for?

The end product is this. Nobody cares about your excuses. Nobody is going to coddle you because you are lazy. It's your butt, you move it. Phones ringing off the hook? I don't want to hear it. Co-worker didn't come to work? I don't want to hear it. Customers upset about their policies. I don't want to hear it. Caught up in the whirlwind, I said that I don't want to hear it.

Nobody wants to hear it. Complaining is not going to get the job done. Whining is not going to get the job done. Making excuses is certainly not going to get the job done. Excuses are the easy way out. You, becoming better at what you do will get the job done. You, becoming an expert in your field will get the job done. You, working harder than you've ever worked before will positively get the job done. The problem is this... most people aren't willing to do what it takes to succeed. So, ask yourself, am I most people?

It's been said, "You can make excuses or you can make money, but you can't do both." The choice is yours. It's all up to you. So, what are you going to do? What serves you best? What serves your family best? If it's excuses then I don't want to hear it. And neither does anyone else.

I was speaking with Felicia Ollie, the HR Director for Shelby County Schools. When her staff begins to complain, she quickly stops them and asks, “So what? Now what?”. She doesn’t want to hear excuses. She wants them to understand that excuses don’t solve anything. Instead, let’s figure out what we’re going to do now. Maybe you should implement this practice in your office, your life, your church, and family. Things didn’t go as planned? So what? Now what? Didn’t hit your goal? So what? Now what? Company making changes beyond your control? So what? Now what? Nobody wants to hear your excuses!

In the book *How to Become a Rainmaker* by Jeffrey J. Fox, a good read for any sales person, there is a great story about excuses. The story goes: A manager captured the attention of his sales force by offering prizes and bonuses for hitting defined sales quotas. The rules were simple; Reach your quota you win, fall short, you lose. Three weeks before the contest deadline an earthquake hit. The sales office was badly damaged and business was interrupted. The sales team did not hit their quota. The sales team wanted the prizes and bonuses but the manager said no. They argued that they missed the goal by only a few points but the manager remained firm. The sales team persisted asking the manager to be reasonable because of the earthquake. The manager responded, "Earthquakes don't count."

Wow…I love this story because this is exactly what this chapter is about. It doesn't matter the circumstances the job still has to get done. Yes, it's noticeably harder but the job still has to get done. Yes, the office is in shambles but it still has to get done. Nobody cares work harder. Now if you're thinking that the manager should have given them the bonuses anyway then once again, you my friend are an excuse maker. You still believe that we should be compensated or rewarded for not completing a task if it isn't our fault or if the excuse is good enough. We will never reach our full potential with this current mindset. The good news is that it's not too late for us to change. Keep reading. Maybe the sales team should have worked harder and faster. Maybe they procrastinated thinking they had enough time. Who knows? It doesn't matter because the end result is that they failed to meet the goal; therefore, no prizes or bonuses should have been paid out. It's funny how most employees have this mindset.

Most employees believe that money grows on

trees. They believe that the employer has a money tree in the back yard. But we are all quick to tell our children that money doesn't grow on trees. We see things in a different light when it comes to our own paycheck don't we? Think about it. If the quota wasn't hit, then the extra money wasn't made. If the extra money wasn't made then how can the manager pay them what was promised. When sales are made the employer gets paid. If they aren't made, no money for anyone. Let's remember that the next time we're complaining about our bonuses or asking for a raise. No sales = No money = No bonuses = No raises.

The story ends with the sales force experiencing another natural disaster the following year. What do you supposed happened? Do you think that they hit their quota or missed it? They absolutely hit it. They were first in the nation. But what if the manager had excepted their excuses the previous year? No doubt they would have not worked as hard during the disaster because they knew that their excuses would have relived them from their duty. But instead they found out that they were tougher, stronger and more capable than they imagined. Making excuses of why we didn't get the job done only makes us weaker, not stronger. Jeffrey J. Fox goes on to say, "You either made the sale or you didn't. No one wants to hear why you didn't bring in the business. No one cares that the dollar was devalued, the economy is lousy, the other guy is cheaper or that your rates have increased. The hunter either comes home with the game or he doesn't. His family eats or goes hungry. No one cares that the rain washed away the deer tracks." You can keep all of your excuses because I don't want to hear it.

NOBODY CARES... WORK HARDER

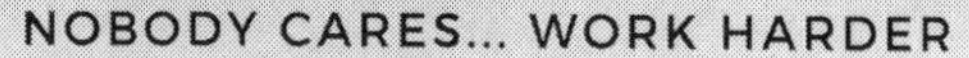

GROW UP!

CHAPTER TWO

GROW UP!

Angel had now spent several years as a successful car salesman. He was now married with a wife and three children. He traded in his bandana and gang colors for a shirt and tie. He was no longer selling your drug of choice, but rather your choice of vehicle, and he was extremely good at it. He managed to move up quickly through the ranks to become the top car salesmen at the dealership. His method was quite simple. People don't walk on the lot unless they want to buy something, so I'm going to sell them something. What if you had that mindset when people called your office or when they came in to see you? Years ago I got into a heated argument with one of my coworkers. They believed that you could help a customer without selling them anything. While I agree with that statement, the ultimate help comes when they need the proper coverage in place…and they have it. Remember, I'm from the insurance industry. If I have a conversation with you about life insurance, answer all your questions about life insurance and run the quotes to see how much life insurance will cost, but I don't sell you the policy, did I really help you? I say no I didn't. I informed you, but I didn't help. Are you simply providing information, or are you actually helping them put the proper coverage in place? I will submit that if that person died without a policy in place, their family would agree that you were no help at all. Yes, I know that you can't make a person buy from you. But unfortunately, most agents and team members don't do a good job of identifying a need. They give up too quickly. They are passive rather than assertive. They are afraid they're going to hurt the customers feelings, so they stay in their comfort zone and no help is provided. Are you informing your customer's or providing genuine help? FYI...the last time I checked, companies don't pay you for informing customers, they pay you for helping them put coverage place. Simply put....Sales! Some of you should go back and read the number one sales book ever written. More on this later. Okay, back to my friend Angel. He was so gifted in the car industry that he soon became the finance manager. He was now overseeing all the deals made on the lot. He was no longer being paid on his actions only, but rather the actions of everyone on the lot.

Billionaires, John D. Rockefeller and Jean Paul Getty, stated that leveraged income is the smartest income there is. Both said, "I would rather make 1 percent on the efforts of 100 people than 100 percent on my own efforts. Do you think it's wise to listen to billionaires when it comes to earning money? Does your income derive from your efforts only? If so, then maybe that's why you aren't where you want to be financially. While we're on the subject, also do your homework on residual income.

Now, can I please get back to my friend Angel? Angel excelled as a finance manager so much that he caught the attention of one of the district managers from a well known bank. After much discussions and several interviews, Angel left the car industry and began wearing a coat to match his shirt and tie as the new bank manager. The district manager immediately began tutoring Angel making sure that he had everything he needed in order to be successful, and he was. Angel inherited a bank that customarily had high turnover and habitually reported low numbers; nevertheless, in standard Angel fashion, he prevailed. Over the next few years he took his branch from last in the district to number one. Soon thereafter he was number one in the three closest districts. Angel was now well known throughout his district and he began to catch the attention of the vice president. On several occasions when the vice president would fly into town to visit the branches, he insisted that Angel accompany the district manager and he at dinner. Things couldn't be better for Angel. A few years later the district manager was now retiring and a replacement had to be chosen. Of course he recommended his protégé Angel for the position. It was more of a formality actually. Angel had been number one for years, he was well known and the vice president (who would be making the decision) liked him. Several branch managers applied for the position and interviews were to be held. The vice president flew in to interview all the candidates. Each interviewee was to be asked a series of questions, all being the same. The decision was to be made immediately and the winning candidate notified. During Angel's interview he answered every question correctly and with confidence. When it was all said and done he was confident that he had gotten the position. But to his amazement, he wasn't chosen.

The vice president took Angel to lunch. After a few minutes into lunch Angel began asking how this was possible? Over the years he'd done everything he'd been asked to do and he was number one at doing it. Although the winner was well qualified, he hadn't put up the numbers that Angel had. The vice president agreed but added, "During the interview there was one very important question that I asked everyone and you were not able to answer it." Angel disagreed, commenting that he had answered every question and answered every question correctly in fact. The vice president reminded him of the question, "During the interview I asked you, what book are you reading, and you didn't have an answer." He went on to explain to Angel that he was looking for someone who was willing to work on themselves just as hard as they were working in their business. If a person continues to work on themselves to become better, then their business, family, life and career will automatically become better as a result. Personal development is the key to all success that is sustained. Angel could not argue. He'd forgotten, even dismissed the one question he couldn't answer. Angel is still number one in the region, still putting up record numbers and still having lunch with the new district manager and vice president when he comes to town. All is the same except for one important thing. When you now ask Angel, "What book are you reading?", his response will be, "*10 to Win* by my good friend Steve Wilmer." Thanks for sharing Angel.

Up until a few short years ago, I was just like Angel. I was not a reader. I spent most of my time working hard all day just to come home, hopefully spend a little time with the family and then sit in my chair and watch my favorite shows. Incidentally, it's been said that wealthy people have large libraries while poor people have large televisions. What size is your library? What size is your television? Is it a direct reflection of your bank account? According to the article "Statistic Brain",

33% of high school graduates will never read a book again. That was definitely me. What's more shocking is that 42% of college graduates will never read another book again either. 80% of American families did not buy a book last year and 70% of us have not even been in a book store in the last 5 years. And if you're saying to yourself, "These statistics don't apply to me because I read." How about this one? 57% of books started aren't even read to completion.

I know people who listen to audio books while driving and I think that's wonderful. It's a lot better than listening to the radio. But for me, there's something about taking notes, underlining things that catch my attention, highlighting certain passages and so on. It also takes discipline and creates a good habit when we're able to slow down, set aside specific time to perform a worthwhile chore like reading. Ten pages a day (of a good personal development book) can change your life. If you can't start with 10 pages then start with 10 minutes. Something is better than nothing. Jim Rohn asserted (If you don't know who Jim Rohn is then you should definitely be reading more) that it isn't what the book costs. It's what it will cost you if you don't read it.

While writing this book I am currently reading *The 15 Invaluable Laws of Growth* by John Maxwell.

This book has inspired me in so many different ways and on so many different levels. During this chapter we will explore a few ideas about growth inspired by John Maxwell and others. I remember my good friend Willie Spears telling me, "Rich people read." It's a very simple but powerful statement. So, what's the opposite of this statement? Poor people don't read. Now when I say poor people I mean those of us who have a means to be able to read. Those of us who have two or three book stores in our community and a public library to boot. Those who choose not to read as I once did. When I say poor, I am referring to those who are living paycheck to paycheck. Those who say, "I have to wait till payday to buy that item." I can speak on this unequivocally because I was one of these people.

One of my favorite acronyms for POOR is Passing Over Opportunities Repeatedly. Poor also means unable to add value to anyone else. A while back I was drinking a flavored water. When my daughter Jayna is around, before I finish she always asks, "Dad can I have the rest?" On this particular day I said, "sure." But when I went to give it to her I realized that I'd drank it all. Bad Dad! I had nothing to give. How many of us live our lives this way? Nothing to give or maybe only a little to give. We can't pour into others unless we have something to pour. Therefore we must fill ourselves up first. Once we empty ourselves out, go fill up again. Repeat this over and over again until God takes us home. Imagine reading a book where the author had nothing to say because there was nothing in him/her to share.

One of the first books that started me on my reading journey is *Twelve Pillars* by Jim Rohn and Chris Widener. This is a great book told in story format. It addresses the twelve pillars that a successful life and career is built on. It's an easy read and not very long. I recommend this book for all adults looking to better themselves in life and business, but I especially suggest that parents purchase this book for their teenagers. Both of my sons have read this book and enjoyed it. Valuable lessons learned at an early age may avoid those mistakes later in life. I won't speak to all the pillars but I will comment on the first. Pillar #1: You must work harder on yourself than you do on your business. This was a real eye-opener for me. Year after year I was just like Angel, working on my business/career but neglecting my personal development, my personal growth. My career was advancing but I wasn't. I was not growing, but rather remaining the same. In my travels I often ask my audience, "How many of you want to grow your business?" All hands undoubtedly are raised. However, when I ask, "How many of you are currently reading a personal development book?" Less than one-third raise their hands. If I ask, "How many are currently listening to some type of personal development audio in their vehicle?" The number dramatically shrinks. And if I ask, "How many of you attended a personal development conference or seminar within the last year?" Only one of two hands are raised. Ask yourself these same questions. Would your hand remain raised? Or would you be like the masses, unable to say yes to these questions.

Listen, don't beat yourself up or feel discouraged. A few short years ago, I was one of those people. I made the decision not to be any longer and so can you. James Allen, author of *As a Man Thinketh*, remarked, "People are anxious to change their circumstances but are unwilling to change themselves; they therefore remain bound." Wow, this quote punched me right in the face. I've had the pleasure of seeing John Maxwell three times in the last three years. Once in my home town of Pensacola, Florida. A second time was from a personal invitation from my friend Brad Murray, who was asked to speak at a Maxwell seminar, and the third was in Houston when Mr. Maxwell was asked to speak at our Zurvita conference (Zeal for Life.) Each time I walked away a bit smarter than I was. Earlier I wrote that when John Maxwell is about to say something strict or unsympathetic, he would first say, "My name is John, and I'm your friend." After the first few times he said this, we began laughing in anticipation of what was to come next. We also leaned forward in our seats ready to take notes because it was certainty going to be beneficial. I currently use this technique from time to time when I'm coaching my clients. It breaks the ice and lets them know that what I am about to say is for their own good and not intended to hurt them.

We all want to hear the truth, even when we know the truth is going to sting a little. As long as it's said with the right motive (to help and not hurt) we must say it. As a marine and having a choleric personality, I know that I can be straightforward and direct at times. It has caused me to ask for forgiveness from my wife Erin on far too many occasions. So now when I'm speaking to an audience during my travels, or at church or even a loved one, I have "borrowed" Mr. Maxwell's saying, "My name is Steve, and I'm your friend." So here it goes, "My name is Steve and I'm your friend." We say that we want a better life, a better business, a better relationship, a better whatever. But the truth is that we really don't. Because if we did, we would do something about it.

Talk is cheap and it's easy to make these statements. The successful person doesn't simply talk about it, they are about it. John Maxwell remarks that the first law of growth is that you must be intentional about it. Growth doesn't just happen. I am intentional about my growth, reading 5-20 pages from a growth book everyday, listening to a growth CD in my vehicle and of course reading and listening to the word of God on a daily basis as well. It's not automatic and if I'm honest with you, I don't want to do it at times. More often I would much rather sit in my chair and watch television. It's much easier to do that. It's much easier to be average, ordinary, normal, regular, common and mediocre (thank you Thesaurus). But I refuse to be average. I want more therefore I must become more. What do you want in life? Are you living an average mundane life or are you living life to the fullest? On a scale of 1-10 where is your family life? Your work life? Your spiritual life? Your financial life? Once again, most people would say that they want more but they are unable to tell you what they are doing to have more or to accomplish more. I hope that you are not one of those people.

If you have been up this point, it's not too late to change. Be intentional about your growth starting NOW! Remember, you cannot change your life until you change something you do everyday. Don't wait, do it now. The longer you wait to do something you know should do now, chances are that you will never do it at all. How does that make you feel?

I can't believe how much I've grown since I wrote *10 to Win* two years ago. My personal growth has accounted for at least a 70% increase my sales. I was more confident and bold after attending a Tony Robbins event. I involved the audience by walking around and calling on people. At times I added some colorful language. The audience was shocked to hear a speaker say, "I'm here to get your ass into shape," but they loved it and responded to it. I approached recruiting prospects differently after attending an Eric Worre event. I wasn't so defensive as I had been in the past. I learned that everyone had a story and that if I would simply listen and relate, I had a better chance of enrolling them as a consultant. John Maxwell taught me how to become a better leader. The speed of the pack is determined by the speed of the leader.

I'm sure that I've spent at least $5,000 on personal development in the last two years. But my revenue has been increased dramatically. I can't keep enough books in stock. I'm constantly selling out every time I speak, and agents are on a waiting list for me to train them. Personal growth works, not to mention that it changes your life. My wife Erin is a twenty-four year retired Navy Chief. She admits that she has drank alcohol since the age of seventeen when joining the Navy. It's when I began my drinking career as well like most veterans.

Well, after attending a Tony Robbins event, she has not had a single drop of alcohol since June 2016. Yes, personal growth absolutely works.

My good friend and mentor Andi Duli observed, "Empty your pockets into your mind and your mind will fill your pockets with gold." So how much have you invested into your personal development? In *Twelve Pillars* Jim Rohn remarked, "Your income seldom exceeds your personal growth." But if I were to ask if you want to earn more money, you would no doubt say yes. Personal development attracts people to you. Prospects and customers want to do business with you because you speak differently, you think differently, you act differently, and you respond differently to their questions. I can't tell you how many sales I've made using quotes and stories from books. I'm confident rather than needy when dealing with prospects. Personal development did that for me. John Maxwell said, "You can't master your career without mastering yourself." How many of you are spinning your wheels trying to grow your business but aren't spending enough time growing yourself? Listen to the experts and start your personal growth journey.

In *10 to Win* I said that goals were important. Goals are great and we all must set and achieve goals.

How else can we know if we hit the mark or not unless we have goals. Let's observe the characteristics of goals vs. growth, "The two G's". Why is growth just as if not more important than goals.

According to Mr. Maxwell, Goals focus on the destination while growth focuses on the journey: I must definitely have a goal in mind, but I can't ignore the journey or the process. Who am I becoming on my way to the goal? What am I learning on my way to the goal? Sometimes the process is hard, but the journey makes us stronger, bigger, better and faster. At times the journey doesn't feel good but it's necessary. The journey requires patience and consistency. That way we truly appreciate the goal once we've achieved it. Why do you think that lottery winners lose everything in a matter of years? Because there was no journey. It was given to them too easily and there was no learning or growing along the way. Don't forsake the journey. Grow!

Goals motivate people while growth matures people: We all want to be motivated. I'm referred to as a motivational speaker. I don't particularly like that title, but I use it so that society will know what I do. If you motivate a fool, you'll have a motivated fool on your hands. We should seek to educate and inspire instead. Motivation lasts but a minute. Maturity lasts a lifetime and is built over a lifetime. We should never stop maturing. Once again, focus on the journey of maturing. It's lifetime of learning rather than a flash in the pan.

Goals are seasonal while growth is lifelong: Basically, we should never stop growing. If we stop growing, we stop learning. We should be reading some type of growth book each day of our lives, or listening to some type of growth audio CD like "Inspired" by Steve Wilmer each day. I "like" certain pages on FB because it helps me grow. We should surround ourselves with those individuals who are smarter than we are on a daily basis because it forces us to grow...or find new friends.

Goals challenge you while growth changes you: Someone once said, "You're either green and growing or ripe and rotting." I want to grow because I want to become a better person. When you make positive changes, positive thing begin to happen. When you begin to grow you can change your paycheck...your zip code... your destiny.

John Maxwell observed that there are things in life that you have to work for and things that you have to wait for. The more you grow you will be able to discern the difference between the two. Some people are waiting for things they should be working for and some are working (in vain) for things they should be waiting for. How will you know the difference if you're not growing? If you're not becoming smarter? If you're not continuously learning? If you're not constantly challenging yourself on a daily basis by doing the simple things that most people won't do. I am reminded of the Serenity Prayer:

> God grant me the serenity to accept the things I cannot change, courage to change the things that I can and the wisdom to know the difference.

As a man of faith, it absolutely bothers me when I hear other people of faith say, "I'm waiting on God." Well, have you ever stopped to think that God is waiting on you? He's already given you everything necessary in order to succeed in life. It's like the old Prego commercial says…"It's in there." So, get up right now and go get it done. Go after what you want. Go after what your creator has ordained for you. Yes, there are some things that we have to be patient for (not my strong suit) but most of our dreams are there for the taking. We just have to get up and go after them. Have faith that God has your back and he will take care of you.

So, I will end this chapter by sharing with you

how I began to grow. The first thing that I did was to cut out so much television. I am convinced that TV is nothing more than an idiot box for the most part, depending on what you're watching of course. There are only a few shows that I will watch. Because I know that I can easily become addicted to television, I purposely won't watch new shows when I hear how great they are. I ask myself, "Is that show going to make me smarter or dumber?" POOR is a state of mind. It means you're unwilling to learn anything new and you're unwilling to think differently. You live inside the box. You're satisfied, comfortable...poor. Here is my own personal kick in the butt story; Years ago I was in Jacksonville, Florida to watch the Jaguars play the Dolphins. After the game a few of us were walking back to the hotel. A guy pulls up in a nice looking black car and asks if we want a ride back to the hotel? It was four of us so we agreed and hopped in. Along the way he began to tell us about this new car service. All we had to do was download this app with the funny name on our smartphone and input our credit card information. He remarked that it was going to change the way people travel and we should invest with them early. We finished our ride, paid him a few bucks and immediately laughed at him once he was gone, because he wanted us to give a total stranger our credit card information. Two years later UBER was everywhere. POOR!

Years ago, I met an elderly gentleman who shared this story with me. When he was much younger he owned an electronics store. A guy came in one day looking for a specific part. He didn't carry the part but inquired what the part would be used for. The guy starts telling him that they are building a system where people will be able to talk on a telephone without any wires being connected to the wall. They were looking for investors and he should jump on it quickly. The elderly gentlemen told me that he literally chased the guy out of his shop because he must have been crazy. Now more people carry cell phones than home phones. POOR!

So, replace TV time with family time. One hour spent with your children is like a lifetime to them. I've also began reading on a daily basis and especially when I travel. I make myself read a few pages each day. Some people will say that they love to read. I don't. I receive great information and revelation when I read but I have to make myself do it. Some people will say that they love to exercise and go running. Stay away from these people for they are crazy. I don't like running or exercising, but I do these things because I realize it's making me stronger and healthier. Reading on a daily basis will do the same for your intellect. I have an accountability partner as well. I have someone to challenge me to become better, someone to ask me, "Did you do your job today?" The checker gets what the checker checks. If there is no accountability, there is a greater chance that we won't accomplish all that we set out to accomplish.

Windshield University is key as well. Listening to an audio CD or audio book is a quick way to build your intellect and grow as well. I'm not saying that it's all work and no play. I still watch television and I still watch sports. But it has drastically decreased over the past few years. Ironically, I have seen my production and my income increase over the last few years. Coincidence? I think not. You get out of life what you put into it. Remember to do today what others won't, so tomorrow you can have what others can't. Don't be simply interested in success, be committed to it. Richard Blanchard remarked, "There's a difference between interest and commitment. When you're interested in doing something, you do it only when it's convenient. When you're committed to something, you except no excuses; only results." So, are you simply interested in growing…or are you committed?

NOBODY CARES... WORK HARDER

GET OFF YOUR BUTT!

CHAPTER THREE

GET OFF YOUR BUTT!

One evening after a long day at the beach, my youngest child Jayna, who must have been around five at the time, asked if she could have a bag of popcorn? I told her yes and that I would fix her a bag in a few minutes. A few minutes turned into thirty minutes and before long Jayna was back asking about her popcorn and this time she wasn't accepting any excuses. She asked if she could pop her own bag like her older siblings were allowed to do. I asked if she knew how and of course she assured me that she did. Fifteen minutes later she returned disappointed with no popcorn. When I inquired about what went wrong, she explained that the microwave was broken. I immediately became upset because with four children in the house things are always broken and no one ever knows how it happened. Distressed, I approached the microwave to assess the situation. Everything looked in order at first glance. I turned it on and it appeared to be working just fine. Puzzled, I asked Jayna to show me what she'd done. I presumed it was operator error. She took the bag of popcorn, put it in the microwave, closed the door and hit popcorn. The microwave began to work as we both watched. But about 20 seconds into it, Jayna opened the door and said, "See it's not working." I smiled and began to explain to her that she had to leave it in the microwave for the duration; how the bag must have consistent heat for the popcorn to pop. After about three minutes of waiting Jayna had a freshly popped bag of popcorn. With a smile on her face she was off to her room to enjoy a movie.

That simple incident got me to thinking. How many of us expect things to happen in our lives without being consistent? How many of us are acting like a six year old, applying inconsistent heat to our business and life, but expecting great results. If we want to achieve greatness on any level and in any area we must be consistent. In *10 to Win*, I remarked that we must be excited about what we do to have success. While I still profess that there is some type of excitement needed to truly take your business and life to the next level, I am confident that consistency plays a much greater role in our success. When I was an insurance producer and I did not hit my goals, I could always track my lack of results back to my inconsistency in speaking with prospects on a daily basis. One reason that excitement has a less tangible value regarding success is that it can't be tracked. You can absolutely track your consistency. As an example, I know that if I speak to six prospects a day,

I can get three or four of them to meet with me, and one or two of them will actually buy from me. By the same token, If I don't speak with six, if I'm inconsistent, then I most likely won't achieve my desired results. Here is the kicker. It doesn't matter if I am excited or not. If I do the work, I will receive the results. There have been plenty of times where I didn't necessarily feel like doing the work, but I did it and received great results. Too many of us are too concerned about how we feel. We have to move past our feelings and get the job done. Now it does help if when I speak with my prospects I am excited and they can hear it in my voice. No one wants to talk to a dull, boring person. Excitement is contagious. But excitement by itself does not get the job done.

Here is one of my favorite quotes:

My name is consistency. I am related to success.
We should hang out more than…
every once in a while.

If I were to ask you if you wanted to be successful in any area you most likely would say yes. But if I were to ask you if you have been consistent in your actions, could you also say yes? Most of us couldn't. Simply showing up for work is not good enough. Simply not quitting is not good enough. Remember that we are talking about success, not survival. Don't simply survive, but thrive. I have been married for nineteen years and like most marriages it hasn't always been easy. But I know for a fact that it would have been a lot easier had I been consistent in my actions. Consistently showing love and consistently going above and beyond to make her feel loved. What about you? What are you doing in your relationship with your spouse or your children or a loved one? Are you consistent? Or are you simply surviving? You can survive on a desert island but it's no fun. Staying in a marriage is the right thing to do. I believe that God has ordained marriage. But we have to be consistent in our actions towards each other.

My wife and I go on several trips per year together. So far this year we've been to New York, New Orleans, Las Vegas, Atlanta, Orlando, Memphis, Chicago and Oklahoma. We are consistent in taking trips together to get away from the hustle and bustle of business. We also do our best to go on date nights and events around Pensacola as well. Now that the kids are older we have a little more freedom. Sometimes we simply lock the bedroom door and won't answer it no matter how many times our kids knock. It gets a little difficult when my youngest is calling my name…but I must remain persistent and consistent in spending that quality time with my wife Erin. By the way men, remember that we were persistent in getting the girl, so now we must be consistent in order to keep the girl. I saw a quote that read, "A man that shows a woman consistency will never have to worry about her loyalty."

You see, consistent action creates consistent results. That works as a negative as well as a positive. If we consistently fail to do the work, then what are the consistent results? It's failure. It's not rocket science. We don't do the work then we wonder why we're receiving these results? Why is business failing? Why are customers leaving? Why is our spouse unhappy? Why are our kids rebelling? My friend Mitchell Price once told me, "Steve, things don't go wrong, they start wrong." So maybe we should start being consistent in our actions if we haven't been.

Author & speaker Willie Spears said that he makes it a point to touch his wife at least twelve times a day. That's right…twelve times a day. He is consistent in doing that. She is consistent in telling him on a daily basis (sometimes in a text) that he is the man; that he is going to do an amazing job wherever he may be speaking. They are consistent in these areas so they can calculate and expect positive results. If they weren't consistent then they could also calculate and expect negative results. Once again, things don't go wrong, they start wrong. So maybe it's time for you to make a new start.

People are always talking about their destiny. Most people see their destiny as something that happens to them. In other words, they believe that they have no control over it. Their attitude is, "Whatever happens is going to happen." The term Que Sera Sera means, "Whatever will be will be." Now for the most part I agree that there are some things that are beyond our control, hence the serenity prayer in the chapter Grow Up. But I absolutely believe that we can shape our destiny by what we do; by who we become. It's not what we do once in a while that shapes our destiny, it's what we do consistently. What is your destiny for your business? What is your destiny for your life? What are your dreams? Are you one of those people who believe that life happens to them? Instead, what if you began to believe that life happens for you rather than to you.

Soichiro was a loyal employee at Toyota; however, he was passed over for an engineering job. He could have thought, "woe is me" but instead he left Toyota and founded his own car company. Today, Honda is worth an estimated 50 billion. Life happened for him, not to him. Blockbuster refused to buy Netflix for 50 million. As a matter of fact, Netflix was literally laughed out of the meeting. Netflix is now worth an estimated 64 billion...and where is Blockbuster? Life didn't happen to them it happened for them. George Bell the then CEO of Excite refused to buy Google for $750,000. Google is now worth an estimated 498 billion, the world's most valuable company, (beating Apple again) and I have never even heard of Excite. Life didn't happen to them it happened for them. I could go on and on but here is my point. Stop playing the victim and realize that God has a plan for your life. He is not surprised by what happens to us. When God closes a door, he opens a window. Are you consistent in looking at the positive or negative in things? Are you consistent in giving up or getting back up when you are knocked down. Personally, I know all too well what it feels like to give up. I want to know what happens when I don't give up. That's why I strive for consistency in life and business.

When I think of consistency I think about habits. Most of us hear the word habit and we immediately think about something negative. But good habits can be built as well as bad habits. Aristotle concluded that we are what we repeatedly do. Excellence, then, is not an act, but a habit. In other words, if we want to obtain excellence in any area, we must become consistent in our actions. We must build good habits. John Maxwell said that we'll never change our life until we change something we do daily. The secret of our success is found in our daily routine. I understand what Mr. Maxwell meant but it's actually not a secret at all. Unfortunately, most people believe that there is a secret to success. But it all boils down to doing those simple daily activities on a consistent basis, building good habits. These habits are easy to do and they're easy not to do as well. That's what really separates the winners from losers in our society. The winners are willing to do the simple things that most others aren't.

Remember the quote, "Everyone wants to shine but no one wants to polish?" Polishing takes work. Polishing will get your hands dirty. Polishing hurts at times. But in the end, it's all worth it. The problem is that no one sees the polishing, they only see the final result. As you know, when I was a young marine I was fortunate enough to be selected as a meritorious corporal. In order to prepare for the board (Interview), I made sure that my uniform was pressed firmly and my boots were shined (back then we wore black boots). I can specifically remember one of the First Sergeants on the panel asking me if I shined my boots personally or if I had someone do them for me. I took great pride in replying, "I did them myself First Sergeant." He remarked, "They look like black glass." He and everyone else saw the end results. No one saw the polishing. No one saw the late nights back and forth with the polish and water over and over again. They didn't see the ripped t-shirts or the permanent black polish stains on my fingers and underneath my nails. They didn't feel the pain of the blood being cut off to my fingers because the t-shirt was wrapped around my fingers so tightly and they didn't know that my fingers hurt for days afterwards. All they saw was the shine. All they saw was the black glass, the end result. Most people won't see your consistency, they will only see your end result. I love the example about what an iceberg really looks like and what people see. We see the tip of the iceberg but actually the majority of it is under water and can't be seen. Success is the same way. The bulk of the work no one ever sees. They only see the tip.

Michael Angier concluded that if you develop the habits of success, you'll make success a habit. The key word here I believe is develop. Good habits are not automatic. We are not born with good habits. They must be developed. What's the best way to develop a good habit? You guessed it, it's consistency. When we do something over and over again for a period of time (some say 30 days) we develop a habit, whether it's good or bad. So, what are your habits regarding your business or job? Take the time to write down what you believe are your good habits. Next to them, write down what you believe to be your bad habits as well. Don't beat yourself up if your second list is longer than your first. Simply make efforts to change those habits. Make efforts to completely delete that second list. If you really want a challenge, ask someone who is close to you to develop the same list for you. See if you come up with the same things. There may be some bad habits that you are blind to. By the same token, there may be some good habits that you possess and don't realize that others see them in you. Do this same exercise for your life as well. What are your good and bad habits when it comes to your family? That may be a tough one to swallow but it will make you better if you're willing to face the truth.

Consistency is an action word. When you think about consistency you think about doing something over and over again. I believe in action. My uncle used to say, "Don't talk about it, be about it." Action speaks louder than words. So don't talk about it, be about it. You want to grow your business? Don't talk about it, be about it. You want to sell more products? Don't talk about it, be about it. You want to have a closer relationship with your family? Don't talk about it, be about it. Anything worth having is worth working for. Talking will only get you so far. It's action that gets you across the finish line. Actions prove who someone is. Words only prove who they want to be. We know that speaking things is powerful, but the next part of that equation is action. We must perform what we speak. Action is the foundational key to all success.

My wife Erin enlisted in the Navy when she was seventeen years old. While the Navy taught her some worthwhile things, it's also where she says that she developed some very bad habits. She remarked that one of those habits was drinking alcohol. In the military, drinking alcohol is somewhat of a right of passage. It's where I had my first drink as well. After attending a Tony Robbins UPW (Unleash the Power Within) event in Dallas, Erin decided that after twenty-nine years she was no longer going to drink alcohol. I remember the night like it was yesterday. It was June 26th on a Sunday night at Houston's restaurant in Dallas, TX. She had her usual glass of wine and said, "This is my last glass.". I'm happy to say that it's been nearly eighteen months and she has not had a single drop of alcohol. Even when surrounded by friends and family members who continue to drink, Erin remains faithful (consistent) to herself. She spoke it, then she did it. Andrew Carnegie said, "The older I get the less I listen to what people say and the more I look at what they do." Action!

We have already established that good habits and consistency may not be easy to do. Do it anyway. There will be times that you simply don't feel like it. Do it anyway. Life will most certainly throw you a curve ball and tell you to put it off till tomorrow. Do it anyway. You will want to quit because you don't see the labor of your fruits. Do it anyway. There will those who say that you're wasting your time. Do it anyway. Keep doing it and doing it and doing it until something happens. Be consistent, develop good habits and never give up. Remember that everything great starts small. Have patience. My niece Cecily told me, "It takes thirteen hours to build a Toyota, but six months to build a Rolls Royce."

Now I also remember a co-worker who was not hitting her goals. She proclaimed to me that she was indeed being consistent on a daily basis, but yet she was still failing. She was in sales and she was consistent in sharing her product with at least three people a day. When I inquired how she was sharing her product she responded, "I tell them the benefits of the product. I then say, you don't want to buy any do you?" Now that's a slight exaggeration but basically, she was consistent in saying the wrong thing. So simply doing something over and over again will not necessarily bring you positive results. Get help on what to say and not to say. Learn how to say it. Consult an expert. Do whatever you have to do in order to succeed. Once you figure out what works, do it consistently over and over again even on the days that you don't feel like it. The universe respects your actions only, not your wishes.

Do it anyway!

NOBODY CARES... WORK HARDER

DIAMOND

CHAPTER FOUR

EVERYBODY WANTS TO SHINE
LIKE A DIAMOND, BUT NOBODY
WANTS TO BE CUT LIKE A DIAMOND

NOBODY CARES... WORK HARDER

DIAMOND

"I believe that we are who we choose to be. Nobody is going to come and save you. You've got to save yourself. Nobody is going to give you anything. You've got to go out and fight for it. Nobody knows what you want except you, and nobody will be as sorry as you if you don't get it."

Now I'm not a Barry Manilow fan but when I saw this quote I was like yes! Finally! Someone speaking right to the core of how I feel, and of all people it was Barry Manilow. I wish that everyone felt this way, but unfortunately most people don't. Most people are happy with accepting the norm, the status quo, being average, accepting what life brings to their door. And then they wonder why they don't have the things in life they desire so much. It's because they haven't worked their butts off to receive it. They sit around waiting for someone else to save them, to come to their rescue, whether it be the government or a family member. It's sad. And you are not doing them any favors if you continue to rescue them. You are actually hindering their growth. I was talking with a good friend of mine who has continued to bail out friends and family over the past years with their finances. He finally understood that if he continued to do so his family and friends would never change their behavior that got them in that situation in the first place. We are where we are in life because of the decisions we've made. So wise up, quit asking for handouts and start making wiser decisions.

Barry says that we are who we choose to be. That is a powerful statement. It means that each one of us has a choice. Once again, we're back to the decisions that we make. It doesn't matter your background or upbringing. It doesn't matter who your parents were or were not. It doesn't matter if you're a woman or man, straight or gay and it definitely doesn't matter what color you are. You still get to choose. You get to choose what you will become. Yes, I agree that it may be more difficult for you in certain situations but so what? Difficult forces you to grow; to become stronger. And if you're stronger, now it's more difficult for others to hurt you. When you're stronger, your loved ones can depend on you. Easy keeps you weak, off-guard, fragile and easily broken, unfortunately like a lot of those in our society. So, stop whining, dig your heels in and get to work. I promise that It will be worth it in the end. Life is not fair. Get over it. I have four children ages 8-16 and they get "popped" if they say those words "Not Fair". As a matter of fact, it does my heart good when I hear my 8yr old daughter tell her older sister, "Get over it Joi, life is not fair." I'm teaching them at an early age what to expect in life. Life will not always go according to plan. You can be the best employee and work your butt off, but the boss' nephew will still recieve the promotion rather than you. Your saying, "It's not fair" isn't going to change the situation. Whining isn't going to change the fact. Fight for what is yours, protest, go to court or find a new job. Action speaks louder than words. Most will simply complain and go back to their desks disgruntle for the next 20 years accepting what life has given them, living a life of mediocrity. That's why I prefer to be an entrepreneur. I determine what I'm worth rather than someone else. I determine if I want a raise rather than someone else. No one can fire me or keep me down. I control my destiny rather than someone else.

I remember hearing about a book called *The Greatest Story Ever Told.* When you open the book it's blank inside because it is intended for you to write your own story. Most let others write their story. The story sounds like this. You will work here, you will earn this amount, you will live in this type of house and you will drive this type of car. You will take this amount of vacations, sick days, etc. You will ask if you can take off to care for a sick child and I will not pay you if you do take off work. As a matter of fact, you have to trade dollars for time. If you work I will pay you but if you don't work I will not pay you. And if I don't like the way that you work, I will find someone else to do this job that I know you hate to do but are too fearful to do what God really intended for you to do. I will decide if you are worthy to receive a raise and I will decide what that amount will be. You will be here for 20, 30 or 40 years and you will retire on 40% of your paycheck. You will die broke, depending on someone else (government & family) to take care of you. And 95% of Americans say...OKAY!

In the book *The Miracle Morning* by Hal Elrod he discusses the 95% reality check. He writes that Approximately 95% of our society settles for far less than they want in life, wishing they had more, living in regret and never understanding that they could be, do, and have all that they want. Hal goes on to quote an extremely sad statistic.

According to the Social Security Administration, if you take any 100 people at the start of their working careers and follow them for the next 40 years until they reach retirement age, here's what you'll find: only 1 will be wealthy; 4 will be financially secure; 5 will continue working, not because they want to but because they have to; 36 will be dead; and 54 will be broke and dependent on friends, family, relatives and the government to take care of them.

We know this is true because we all know someone in this situation right now. Most people are broke, living from paycheck to paycheck, unwilling to do anything about it or unwilling to find out how to do anything about it. They simply accept life as it comes. Are you one of those people? Which number in the above statistic will you be; wealthy, financially secure, still working or dead broke? The choice is yours.

Manilow says that no one is going to come and save you. You've got to save yourself. I had an elderly man tell me once, "I don't believe in social security, I believe in self security." How fitting is that. He's not going to put his trust, his financial security in someone else. Because no one is going to come and save you. Too many people sit around asking for handouts. They put their hope in others to take care of them. As a little black boy growing up on welfare, I saw how the system was abused and we see it today. I don't believe in a handout, but I do believe in a hand-up! We should help those around us until they are able to help themselves.

And it's not just the welfare program I'm talking about. There are those with jobs who ask for handouts as well. Have you ever asked your employer for a raise, yet your production remained the same? Ask yourself, what type of value do I bring to the company? Am I encouraging those around me or draining them? Do I show up for work early and stay late? Do I go above and beyond or simply do the bare minimum? As I quoted Jim Rohn in an earlier chapter, "Your income seldom exceeds your personal growth." When we become more, we can expect more. Why is it that most employees expect a raise for doing their job, for doing what they were hired to do? It's like giving children a participation trophy when they lose. You didn't get the job done, but rather than work harder, here's a reward. No wonder we have minimum wage employees asking for $15hr to do a job that requires minimum skills. Don't get me started on that.

Most say, "Pay me more money because I need it. I want it. Pay me $15hr without requiring me to learn any new skills to warrant a pay increase." Barry says, "No one is going to give you anything. You've got to go out and fight for it." Most don't want to fight. They don't want to grind. They want it to come to them on a silver platter. They complain. Once again Author and Speaker Jim Rohn remarked, "Don't wish it were easier, wish you were better." If you were better, you would earn more. Personal growth is a major key. In my last job I was most likely the highest paid employee for that company in Northwest Florida. Most would have settled. Most would have stayed. But my personal development would not allow me to settle. I wanted more. I quit my job and started my own speaking company. I now earn twice as much as I did working for someone else. And this is just the beginning.

I will be a millionaire in the next two years or sooner. MARK MY WORD!! But most don't want to become better. Don't be like most. Go out and fight for what you want. Don't take no for an answer. Be assertive, be confident, be a little pushy if you must, but get the job done. Finally, my friend Barry (oh yes, he's definitely my new best friend) says that no one knows what you want, and no one will be more disappointed than you if you don't get it. I believe that's the reason so many people are unhappy these days. Tony Robbins says that they are "suffering" so they want others around them to "suffer" as well. We know these people. It's the coworker that everyone avoids because they always have a bad attitude. It's the person behind the counter that's "short" with you when all you did was ask a simple question. Maybe it's the relative that the family doesn't want to invite over for the holidays because they would ruin everything. And if no one came to mind in the above examples I just gave, then you are one of these people. When people are unhappy they want to make everyone else unhappy. My wife says, "Hurt people, hurt people" meaning people who are hurting tend to hurt others." So, go after what you want. Live your dream. Do something that makes you happy. If not for you, then for the rest of us who have to put up with your suffering.

What about when people say, "I'm doing my best. I'm doing all I know how to do. Well learn how to do something differently. Get some help, consult an expert. Google it. Your best may not be good enough to get the job done. Your best quite frankly may suck. It's funny how we use "I'm doing my best" as an excuse for failing, and we expect a pass. But most of us would never accept that if the shoe was on the other foot. You dropped my burger on the floor, it's okay, I know you're doing your best. You put onions on my burger in the drive-thru and I didn't realize it until I got all the way home. I'm not upset, you're doing your best. My cable bill was twice as high this month because the promotions ended, and you didn't call to tell me? No problem, you're simply doing your best. No more hiding behind "your best". Do better. Steve, you totally screwed this up. "You're right, I'll do better." Steve, your production was short this month. "I know, I'll do better." If your best is not cutting it, then get some help, find a new way of doing it, or find a new profession. If you want to be successful in any area of your life or business you have to do what's necessary. Ask yourself, "Am I really doing what's necessary to succeed? Am I truly giving it my all? Most likely, if we're honest with ourselves the answer is no. Remember what I said earlier, "Don't be upset with the results you didn't get from the work you didn't do." But if the answer is yes, then don't give up. Dig in deeper. What comes easy won't last. And what lasts won't come easy. So, don't you dare give up.

"You have three choices, Give up... Give in... or Give it all you've got"

I sometimes sing karaoke and believe it or not I have a few favorite country songs I like to sing. From Garth Brooks to The Charlie Daniels Band. One of my all-time favorites is by Tim McGraw. The title of the song is "How Bad Do You Want It?" In the song, Tim says that people always ask him what it takes to reach out and touch their dreams. His answer is simple. He asks, "Are you hungry? Are you Thirsty? Is there a fire that burns you up inside? How bad do you want it? How bad do you need it? Are you eating, sleeping, dreaming with that one thing on your mind? Because if you want it all, you've got to lay it all out on the line." Most of us haven't laid anything on the line. We say we want it badly but our actions (lack of actions) prove otherwise. Talk is cheap. The universe doesn't grant wishes to those who simply ask. Massive Action must accompany your ask. Are you eating, sleeping, dreaming with that one thing on your mind? Or when you clock out, does your dream clock out as well. What you think about and focus on most always becomes your maximum potential. So change your focus and you'll change your potential. Most of us are comfortable. We say we want more but the truth is that unless it begins to hurt, we won't do anything about it. My wife and I were having this conversation just today about our health. We are getting our eating habits under control before it begins to hurt. Before the doctor says, "You've been diagnosed with __________" People living from paycheck to paycheck are comfortable because at least they have a paycheck. If they want more they have to do more and most don't want to put in the extra work.

The story goes like this…There was a homeless man standing on the street corner with his dog sitting next to him. As I slowed my vehicle to give him a few dollars I noticed that his dog was howling. I inquired, "What's wrong with your dog?" He replied, "He's sitting on a nail." I asked, "Why won't he get up off of the nail?" His response, "I don't know. Maybe it's not hurting him bad enough." Wow, what a revelation. How many of us sit on a nail every single day? We complain about things but are unwilling to do anything about it. We whine and cry about what we don't have, what we wish we had, how tough things are financially but we won't get up off that nail. We go to the same dead-end job day after day hoping by some miracle that things will change. But what did Barry say? He plainly said that no one is going to save you. You've got to save yourself. So, figure out what you've got to do to have what you want. Sometimes I sit up late at night asking myself (and God) am I doing all that I can? The answer is always no! So, I figure out what needs to be done and start doing it. If I don't have the answer I get the answer from someone who is succeeding in that area. I get advice from an expert. Ask yourself, are you doing all that you can? If you're honest with yourself, and you might as well be, the answer is probably no. That means that you have no one to blame for where you are in life except yourself. This is your life and you are responsible for your results. No one else, only you. Put that in your pipe and smoke it. Or choke on that for a while.

Patrick Bet-David, author of *25 Laws for Doing the Impossible*, commented, "Most people are very concerned about being embarrassed, being humiliated and failing." They worry about people saying, "You were a failure, you couldn't do it, I told you so. They struggle with these things. That is tough for them. So, because of that, they play life…very, very safe." I totally agree with this. It wasn't safe for me to leave a guaranteed paycheck. I was comfortable where I was. But there is danger in the comfort zone.

Once I began working on myself I became uncomfortable and had to do something about it. Most people are paralyzed by what others think of them, by what others are going to say. I used to be this way years ago. And sometimes I catch myself feeling this way at times today but I quickly snap out of it. As an example, I am a huge believer in the profession of Network Marketing. It's how I got my start in sales and it has trained me and prepared me for my current business. It's a major reason that I am successful today in speaking. It's a major reason that I was successful in insurance sales. If you can become successful in the network marketing profession, I am convinced that you can do almost anything. So, because I don't care about what others think of me I succeed. They may say it's a pyramid scheme.

That's their ignorance talking, they don't understand. It's hard to hear opportunity knocking if you're always busy knocking the opportunity. POOR!
FYI…broke and skeptical is a bad combination.

They don't pay my bills anyway so what does it matter. Most of them (the naysayers, dream killers, dream stealers, scoffers) are not financially free anyway. So, what do they know? I have friends who earn $300k-$1M a year in MLM. They live life on their own terms, no one telling them when to come and go, no quotas, no bosses and no employees. They don't have to be anywhere they don't want to be, and they answer to no one. They come from all different backgrounds and all different education levels. I don't know ANYONE who makes that kind of money with those same benefits.

What is it that you want to do but are worried about what others will say? Most of those people simply want to keep you from becoming more. They want you to remain the same because if you change, it may force them to change. If you become better, then you may leave them. You may move on and find new friends. So rather than have that happen, they discourage you or mock what you are doing. Are you going to let them steal your dream? Are you going to succumb to their fears? Why are you playing life safe? Why are you accepting what life gives you rather than going out and getting what you want? What are you afraid of? You are never going receive everything that God has for you staying inside your little comfortable box. Someone else is going to get it. Looking foolish is the price of admission if you want to improve. Listen, if you never want to fail, be embarrassed or afraid, then say nothing, do nothing, become nothing. But don't complain about it when you see life passing you by. Don't be upset at the CEO who received a huge bonus last year. Don't ask for handouts from those who got off their butts and did the work. You made the choice, now live with it.

Are you waiting or working? Ok, are you working your butt off? Ok, are you working your butt off doing what you love to do? Gotcha!! Most of you are able to answer yes to "working your butt off. But when you throw in "doing what you love to do, or doing what you're born to do, you stumble. Friends (I know that by now it doesn't seem as if I'm a friend, but I am) I know this all too well because I was there, and now I want to help as many people as possible. One company refused to hire me as a speaker after reading my book. The reason given was that they didn't want me telling their employees to follow their dreams. They were afraid that the employees might just do that…and quit. They wanted to keep nice quiet little employees who did what they were told. Employers, what type of production do you think you receive from someone who doesn't want to be there in the first place? How about encourage your people to become better? If they feel better about themselves and their lives they make better employees. And if they decide to leave and pursue other venues, then they weren't meant to be there in the first place. You can't keep someone who doesn't want to be kept. Remember the old saying, "If you love someone let them go. If they return, they were always yours. If they don't they never were." God has for you who is for you. Nothing or no one can change that.

CFO says to the CEO: What if we invest money, time & resources into our people and they leave? CEO responds: What if we don't, and they stay?

Isaiah Hankel concluded, "The world doesn't owe you happiness, health, love, respect or money. The world owes you nothing. You are where you are because of your decisions, not because of your circumstances. Stop whining and stop being bitter. Take responsibility for yourself. Be big enough to say, this is my life,

I'm responsible for it and I'm going to make something of it." Ouch, that hurt. Yep, the world owes us nothing. We've already been given everything we need to succeed in this life. Society has gotten to the place where everybody has a right, but everybody doesn't have a responsibility. Image what kind of country we would have if everyone took responsibility for their own actions. No excuses just responsibility. A lot of the people that I train blame their company for not being able to make more sales because of rate increases. They complain that a cheaper company is taking their customers. They whine about the customers not wanting to come in to meet with them. You name it they have an excuse.

Like I said earlier, nobody cares, work harder. Didn't hit your numbers this month? Nobody cares, work harder. Your company changed the compensation plan? Nobody cares, work harder. Transferred to a new area and you don't know anyone? Nobody cares, work harder. Had to fire your team and start over? Nobody cares, work harder. No one wants to hear excuses, we want results. We don't want to be told why it didn't get done, we want to hear that it was done, and that it was done well. Your mortgage company doesn't accept excuses, they want their money. Bill collectors don't accept excuses, they want their money. Your excuse, my excuse, everyone's excuse is invalid. As I've said over and over again, "When I lost all of my excuses, I found all of my results." And excuses don't hide you. They only reveal who you really are. The same boiling water that softens the potato hardens the egg. It all depends on what you're made of. What are you made of? What do you do when things get tough? What do you do when the water begins to boil? Will you become soft or hard? Choices!

There is an old African proverb. It reads, "Every morning in Africa a gazelle wakes up. It knows that it must run faster than the fastest lion, or it will be killed. Every morning a lion wakes up. It knows that it must run faster than the slowest gazelle or it will starve to death. It doesn't matter if you are a lion or a gazelle, when the sun comes up you had better be running."

This should be our attitude on a daily basis. In your business you had better be running. In your marriage you had better be running. At your job you had better be running. In all that you wish to accomplish you had better be running. No days off; There is no finish line. One of my favorite motivational speakers Eric Thomas says, "Success and Nothing Less." Now you say it loudly, "Success and Nothing Less." What? Are you worried that people will look at you funny? Worried that you will sound stupid? Worried what others will think about you? It's called a declaration, a formal explicit statement or announcement. You are making this announcement, this statement over your life. SAY IT!!! SUCCESS AND NOTHING LESS!

Take it day by day. Every morning when you wake up and your feet hit the floor say it again, "Success and Nothing Less." Throughout the day whether things are going well or not so well say it anyway, "Success and Nothing Less."

Get up, dust yourself off, dry your eyes, stop feeling sorry for yourself, quit whining and complaining and get back in the game. Yea I know it hurts but who cares, work harder. Don't quit, don't give up and don't take no for an answer. Figure it out. There's always another way. Go after what you want and don't stop until you get it. You can't be stopped. It's morning time and your gazelle is waiting for you…

What are you going to do?

NOBODY CARES... WORK HARDER

DON'T BLAME ME!

CHAPTER FIVE

DON'T BLAME ME!

"Improper planning on your part does not constitute an emergency on my part."

This is one of my favorite quotes. It basically says that just because you didn't do what you were supposed to do…don't blame me. If you didn't plan properly and now things in your life are all jacked up, don't blame me. If it was your responsibility to get the job done…and you didn't, don't blame me. In the world that we live in it appears that we are always looking for someone else to blame, someone else to take the fall, someone else to hold responsible for our actions or inactions. We never want to take responsibility for our own short-comings and failures. It's never our fault, it's always someone else's. It aggravates me when I hear that someone hurt another person because they were abused as a child, or bullied as a child. I'm not making light of the situation and I understand that these things affect us in life. Even after we've become adults we may still carry the hurt that was once done to us. But once we become an adult it's time to make adult decisions. It's time to take responsibility for our own actions. We can no longer blame others for the things that we've done.

We would all be so much further on in life if we simply stopped blaming others. Earl Nightingale said that we are exactly where we want to be in life whether we will admit it or not. There is so much truth in this statement. Of course, I know that things may happen to us beyond our control but remember that life is 10% of what happens to us and 90% of how we respond. The world is full of people who were dealt a bad hand and still make the best of it. They actually triumph.

I'm reminded of a speaker that I saw in my hometown by the name of Nick Vujicic. He was born with no arms or legs, yet he is changing lives with his inspirational words and messages. He doesn't blame anyone. Speaker Erik Weihenmayer is blind but he climbed Mt. Everest. He doesn't blame anyone for being blind. Now you are probably thinking that these are physical disabilities and it's different when someone mistreats you or attempts to hold you back or hold you down. You still have no one to blame. Yes, there are those out there who will do everything in their power to keep you down. It's your job in life to do everything to keep them from succeeding. Some don't want to see you succeed or they only want you to succeed as long as it doesn't threaten their job or status. It doesn't matter, you still can't blame them.

Remember, nobody cares work harder. Sometimes you may have to do twice the work to receive the same pay. It's been documented that women in the workplace usually receive less money than their male counterparts. It's not right…but it's life. Until things change we must work harder. We must go the extra mile; perform above and beyond. One of my favorite speakers Eric Thomas say, "You may be smarter, but you will not outwork me." Imagine the commitment and work ethic that must take. He says, "You will not beat me to the spot." I love that mindset. I have adopted that mindset as well. I totally get where Eric is coming from. I know that I'm not the smartest of my peers. I barely graduated high school. But why am I enjoying a successful life most of them are not? Why were my sales numbers higher? Because you will not outwork me. You will not beat me to the spot. Do you have that mentality? How hard are you willing to work? Are you beaten to the spot on a daily basis? Then run faster. Train harder and become quicker.

Speaker Jim Rohn said that he could win any sales contest, even if he wasn't that good at sales. The top sales person sales 100 widgets. How did they do it? They talked to three people and sold one widget. So, talking to 300 people would get them to 100 sales. Jim said that since he knew that his closing ratio was 5 to 1, he would have to talk to 500 people just to receive the same results as the top sales person. So, if he talked to over 500 people he would win the contest. How? He was willing to put in the work. Just like Eric said, "You will not outwork me." Most people would say they lost because they aren't as good as others. It doesn't matter. Do the extra work. Don't blame your lack of skills on why you didn't succeed. Become better. Learn something new. Read a book. Get help. Do something differently besides placing the blame on someone or something else. Jim also says, "Don't wish it were easier, wish you were better." This is so true because most people want it easy.

Most insurance agents and their staff are complaining about insurance rates being so high, that it is nearly impossible to sell auto insurance. They are not lying. The rates are higher than they've ever been. Most consumers don't understand that cheaper is not better. They have been taught that price is the most important thing, so I understand that it's more difficult these days. But blaming your inability to meet your goals on rate increases is not the answer. It works just the way that Jim said. When prices were less you could talk to 3 and sell 1. Now that prices are rising you may have to talk to 5 or 10 to sell 1. I'm not saying that it's easy, but I am saying that it's possible, if you're willing to put in the work. Take responsibility and get the job done. Winston Churchill observed, "The price of greatness is responsibility." Everyone wants to be great. No wants to be average. But very few are willing to put in the work to obtain greatness. They would rather blame their inability to succeed on something other than themselves. What actually happened was that someone beat you to the spot. Someone outworked you. What's sad is that most are ok with it. I hate losing. I would go so far as to say that I'm a sore loser. I don't kick and scream or act ugly when I lose (I rarely lose) but I hate losing. Some people don't mind. And those people tend to lose over and over again. They develop a losing habit. Famed football coach Vince Lombardi remarked, "Winning is a habit, unfortunately so is losing." What type of habit are you developing?

My wife Erin is a retired Navy Chief Petty Officer and currently a financial advisor with Edward Jones Investment. On a few occasions she has had clients move their money from her branch because of the color of her skin. Their exact words were, "We didn't know you were black." So, what do you think she did? Did she sit down and cry about it? Did she blame the company? Did she quit or give up? No, she didn't. She dug her heels in and made up in her mind that she was going to work extra hard to succeed. She didn't cry about it because crying about it would do no good. She knows that she has to work extra hard for her clients because she realizes that there are those out there who have certain stereotypes about people. It is what it is. Blaming someone else for the situation that you are in never works. Most of the time (not all the time) it's our own fault that we are in the situation in the first place. I often ask people who complain about not having enough money if they want to earn more money? Everyone says yes. Then I ask, "Why aren't you earning more money?" They say things like, "My company won't give me a raise, or my company makes it hard to sell our product." They blame the company or someone else rather than themselves. It's never their fault. Listen to me, with this kind of thinking you will never amount to much in life.

You must learn to take responsibility for your success in life as well as your failures. It's not always going to be fair but blaming others is a waste of time. It's unproductive and doesn't generate anything positive. Remember, my kids are not allowed to say, "It's not fair." Do you find yourself using those words; "It's not fair?" Welcome to life. Get over it. Do something about it or quit complaining. No one wants to hear your whining. If you feel that you are being mistreated; If you believe that your rights have been violated; If you want someone to stand up and take notice, then by all means take the appropriate actions to change the situation. I'm not saying that you should lie down and take whatever is given to you. I would never do that, and I wouldn't expect anyone else to either. We all have choices in life. You can try to change the situation, quit and go to another company, start your own company or bear and grin it. But don't blame others and please no whining. By the way, those who quit will most likely end up facing the same situation at the next job. It's not the job or the situation. Most of the time it's them.

There is a powerful video that I saw on Facebook. Allow me to set the scene. A teacher had his students all line up for a race. The prize for the winner was a brand new one hundred-bill. Of course, they were all excited. It was a mix of teenagers, boys and girls, black and white. Everyone was standing on line together ready to go. But then the teacher began to give some odd instructions. He said things like, "If your parents are still married take two steps forward. If you had a father-figure in the home take two steps forward. If you never had to worry about where your next meal was coming from take two steps forward, etc." This went on for a few minutes. By the time he finished asking the questions the students were all over the place. Some had a major head start on the others. There were actually a few students still standing on the starting line. The teacher explained that this was an example of life. There are those who have a head start right from the beginning and they had nothing to do with it. There are those who were further behind than others and they had nothing to do with it either. The comments went back and forth. Some agreed with the video and some disagreed. As I listened to the video I realized that if I were in that race, I would still be on the starting line. Anyone who doesn't believe that there are those of us who have a head start in certain areas are simply in denial. But like the teacher said, "The ones standing on the starting line still have to run their own race." They don't get to blame their parents or their upbringing or anything like that. They may be starting behind everyone else, but they still have to run this race called life. Nobody cares about your upbringing when it's time to pay the mortgage. No one is going to give you a break when it's time to put food on the table. It's your responsibility.

I know that I started behind (and ahead) of a lot of people. I have to run my race. So, I run just a little bit faster than my counterparts. I don't stop to rest as much as others may. As a matter of fact, when I cross the finish line I keep running. Keep your $100, I'll get my own. I'll get $200, $500, $1,000. I will run as far as the eyes can see. I'm not blaming my mother for having us live in projects. I'm not blaming my dad for not being in my life. I'm not blaming anyone because my life is my responsibility, and no one else's. We are not a product of our circumstances, we are a product of our decisions. The sad part is that there were kids on the starting line that didn't even try. They stood there because they figured that there was no chance of them winning that $100. They said, "It's not fair, so why bother?" They gave up without ever trying. Let the record show that you hit a home run. Let the record show that you struck out. But don't let the record show that you didn't take a swing. You must take a swing at this thing called life.

Things may be hard at times. So, you're allowed to scream, you're allowed to cry, but you're not allowed to give up. You're not allowed to throw your hands in the air and say, "To heck with it all." It hurts my heart when I hear about someone who committed suicide. I had a good friend of mine commit suicide two years ago. It's always a difficult thing to deal with. Always remember that God has a purpose for your pain, a reason for your struggle, and a gift for your faithfulness. So don't give up.

I never blame others for my failures or my inability to achieve the goal. I believe that most of our failures can be traced back to it being our fault; a decision that we made. If you're the type of person who doesn't agree with that statement, then you're most likely the type of person who blames others. I made this statement in a study group once. A lot of people agreed with me but there were two people in particular who did not agree; so, we put it to the test.

One person was somewhat homeless (living with friends) because she had lost most of her possessions in a tornado. All eyes were on me to answer. I simply asked, "What did you do with the $50,000 from your renter's insurance?" Her response was, "I didn't have renter's insurance." So, you made a choice not to have insurance that would've protected your things. She then said that she really didn't know what renter's insurance was all about. I responded, "So you chose not to find out about this policy that could have protected all your things?" She then said that she probably couldn't afford it anyway since money was tight. I responded, "So you choose to work at a place where you don't earn enough money?" Everything she said I was able to show her how it was her choice. She didn't like it at all, but my point was made. I believe that if she had taken that example and admitted that it was her responsibility, then she would have made a shift in her thinking and possibly her life would have turned around. But because she refused to take responsibility for her inactions, she will remain the same. Everything in your life is a reflection of a choice that you have made. If you want a different result, make different choices. Most people would learn from their mistakes if they weren't so busy denying them.

I invite you to think about the failures in your life. The times that you missed the mark. You can probably see it was because of a decision that you made. We have no one to blame but ourselves. The sooner we accept that, the better off we'll be. Speaker Les Brown remarked, "If you take responsibility for yourself you'll develop a hunger to accomplish your dreams." Do you have a hunger to accomplish your dreams? Do you have any dreams? Or have you given up on your dreams like most adults? It's time to dream again. It's time to stop making excuses and stop blaming others for your failures.

While we're talking about failures please remember that failure is not the opposite of success. It is a part of success. Every great success story has failure in there somewhere. Did you know that Thomas Edison's teacher told his mother that he was too stupid to learn anything? He was expelled, and his mother had to teach him at home. He went on to become the inventor of the century. Michael Jordan was cut from his high school basketball team. His coach said he lacked talent. He went on to become one of the best basketball players in NBA history, winning six championship titles and eventually owning an NBA team himself. Walt Disney was fired from his newspaper job for lacking imagination. He went on to build the Disney brand including Disneyland and Disney World. Oprah Winfrey was fired from her job as a reporter because she was unfit for television. She became the #1 talk show host in television history and now has her own television network. Steve Wilmer barely graduated high school with a 1.9GPA and was told by his teacher that he would never amount to anything. He now owns two businesses and is on track to becoming a millionaire in the next few years.

Taking responsibility for exactly where you are

gives you the power to be exactly where you want to be. When we begin to take responsibility for our actions we tend to make wiser decisions because we know we'll have no one to blame but ourselves if things don't go right. So, no more blaming others for what didn't go right in your life. Take responsibility and start making wiser decisions today.

But whatever you do...
Don't Blame Me!

NOBODY CARES... WORK HARDER

OXYGEN

CHAPTER SIX

NOBODY CARES... WORK HARDER

OXYGEN

I was broke, living from paycheck to paycheck, for a long time. Actually, that has been my story for most of my adult life. While we're on the subject of broke, here is what I mean. If you have to wait till payday to purchase something, then you my friend are broke. There were times when I needed to make a $200 purchase, or the car broke down or a friend needed money (because broke people associate with other broke people) and I had to wait till payday. I saw a statistic once that reported 7 out of 10 Americans are living from paycheck to paycheck. Most of us know those 7 people. Most of us are or have been those 7 people. I definitely was one. But the reason that I was one of those 7 was because I made excuses and I made poor financial decisions. I blamed my inability to succeed on anything else other than me. I said things like, "If I'd had someone to teach me about finances, then I wouldn't be in this situation, or if I made more money I wouldn't be in this situation. If I had a better job, then I wouldn't be in this situation. If the government…If my boss…If my dog…blah, blah, blah. Excuse after excuse after excuse.

I went from being in the 7 out of 10, to earning

more money than ever before, having more cash on hand than ever in my life and an almost perfect credit score. I own 2 successful businesses and I'm on track to purchase a company that will do a million dollars in revenue this year. Why? Because I stopped making excuses and started making better financial decisions. I started surrounding myself with others who make better financial decisions. The conversation is different when speaking with a millionaire. It's the subtle things that you pick up. It's the mindset that they have; the financial decisions that they make. It's where they spend their money, how they spend their money, when and why they spend their money and why not spend the money. For the most part they don't live flashy and brash lives. They live beneath their means, not trying to impress anyone. Growing up in my culture, it's all about impressing others and keeping up with the Joneses.

When I started my first business years ago, I wanted to buy a brand-new Lexus. I had a small taste of success and I wanted to show it off. My financial advisor and good friend Joel told me not to do that. He said that it would be more impressive to have $40,000 of investments that are growing rather than a $40,000 car that's depreciating in value each month. So, of course, I listened to the expert, right? Wrong! I bought the $40,000 car and spent the next six years trying to pay that beast off, constantly refinancing, trying to obtain a lower price when my growing business came to a halt. I kept that Lexus for another five years, eleven years in all. I would still have it today if the engine had not blown. It took me a while, but I learned. I trained myself to buy assets and not buy liabilities. I'm still learning. Now we have an expert on finances in our home.

My wife Erin is a successful financial advisor with Edward Jones. She makes sure that our assets continue to grow. When the engine blew on my Lexus, I was forced to go car shopping. It felt great not having to make a car payment for years. My first decision was not to purchase a new vehicle. Keep in mind that at this point in my life, God has blessed me to be able to purchase almost any vehicle that I choose. I went to the lot and passed over all the luxury vehicles with the high price tags. I settled on a modest American made vehicle. It's nice, comfortable, plenty of room for the boys in the back seat (they're growing so fast) and the price was perfect.

When my friend Joel saw the vehicle he jokingly remarked, "I'm proud of you. You're growing up." Yea, but it took me nearly forty years to make that turn. Better late than never I guess. There are those who still haven't turned that corner, those who still make financial missteps. I'm constantly talking to my boys about finances and spending. Josiah saves just about every penny that he earns. He always has money. Remember that I don't give my boys an allowance or pay them for doing chores or for getting good grades. We provide food, shelter and school tuition so chores and good grades are expected. I pay them for self-education. I pay them $10 or $20 for every self-education book that they read. They must write a synopsis of the book and then we discuss it. There is no limit to the amount that they can earn. If they do the work, they can earn as much as they want. This has already begun to pay huge dividends. Their conversations and way of thinking are totally different (well not totally) from the average fifteen-year old. My son Josiah asked me one day, "Dad, why doesn't school teach you about real life, stuff like credit cards, taxes and business expenses?" I told him that I agreed and that our education system hasn't changed in over 100 years. Everything else around us is evolving and the school system remains the same.

Another reason that I pay them for the books they read is that I'm teaching them to be paid your worth rather than let someone else determine your worth. You be in control of your destiny and your finances. If you read books, you'll be paid. The more books you read the more you'll earn. It's up to you rather than someone else. Ask Judah or Josiah what's the highest paid profession and they both will tell you that it's sales--trading goods and services for money. Most people hate sales because it's too hard, and of course most people don't want hard. They want easy. That's why it's so simple to outshine others in our society. Most have a mediocre mindset and are looking for easy. Jim Rohn said that he teaches kids to have two bicycles, one to ride and one to rent. It's never too soon to start their training. They won't learn this in school.

Go Pro Event founder Eric Worre remarked, "Our educational system is mostly an employee farm. It's where you grow good little employees. Stay in line, raise your hand, sit still, think like this, do what you're told or there will be consequences. There is a vast difference between having an employee mindset and entrepreneur mindset. The employee puts in work for two weeks and says, "Where's my paycheck? Pay me for the time I have given you." The entrepreneur understands that they will not be paid (or underpaid) for a certain time to be overpaid for an unlimited amount of time. New York Times best-selling author and multi-millionaire Robert Kiyosaki demonstrates this philosophy in his book Rich Dad/Poor Dad. His college-degreed, highly educated father was poor but his friend's father who did not have a degree, but was an entrepreneur was rich.

Robert also demonstrates this philosophy in his simple but powerful explaination known as the cash-flow quadrant. On the left side of the quadrant you have the poor. On the right side of the quadrant you have the rich. LEFT SIDE: You have the E's. E stands for employee. Their mindset is: I'm looking for a safe and secure job with benefits. They usually work for 40+ years, retire on 40% of what they were making and struggle financially in their later years. You also have S's. These are your mom & pop small business, or one man show. Their mindset is: If you want it done right, do it by yourself. They believe that they own their business but actually they don't. It's been said that if you can't walk away from your business and it still continues to grow, then you don't own your business. Your business owns you. RIGHT SIDE: You have the B's. B stands for big business. Their mindset is: I'm looking for the smartest people I know to help run my company. They are not alone. They understand the power of leveraged income; earning money from other's efforts.

You also have the I's. I is for Investor. These individuals make their money work for them rather than them working for their money. On the LEFT SIDE is 95% of our population but only owns 5% of the wealth, while the RIGHT SIDE is 5% of the population but owns 95% of the wealth. Which side are you on? If you don't like your answer, are you doing anything to change it?

What are you teaching your children?

Go to college	Is college for you?
Get a job	Become an entrepreneur
Get married	Work your butt off
Go into debt	Buy assets, not liabilities
Have kids	Marriage & kids
Work to pay off debt	Travel & have fun
Retire at age 65	Retire at age 45
DIE	LIVE

So which plan from above are you currently on? Like Dr. Phil says, "How's that working out for you?" Whenever I speak to teenagers, which I'm not a big fan of doing, they always perk up when we discuss making money. One of the things that I suggest to them is to take a look at their parents. If their parents are wealthy or financially free, then do what they did. Learn from them. If they're not, then do the opposite. It's that simple.

This chapter is entitled Oxygen because of Zig Ziglar and Rita Davenport. Both are well known speakers in their own rights. They stated, "Money isn't everything, but it ranks up there with oxygen." Try living your life without oxygen and see how far you make it. You begin to gasp for air, clutch at your chest, panic, pass out and eventually die. Not having enough money can make you feel like you're experiencing similar symptoms. At times it's hard to breathe; we feel like we're going to pass out and eventually we do die…a financial death. The encouraging news about a financial death is that you can recover from it if you know what you're doing. That's why I'm writing this chapter. It's not that I have it all together and have all the answers. I'm letting you know where I came from, where I am now, and where I'm going. There is no reason that you can't do the same thing. But the sad truth is that most reading this book won't change anything. That's okay…that's why it's so simple to outshine most people remember?

What do others say about money? We hear things like, "Money isn't everything or money can't buy happiness or money is the root to all evil." All of these statements are false. In fact, these statements are mostly uttered by those who don't have enough money or on occasion those who have a lot of money, maybe to ease their conscience for something. These statements are used to rationalize or justify their failure to have money. Obviously, money isn't everything. Our salvation ultimately is everything. The Bible says that you cannot serve both money and God, but It also says that money answers all things. I'm not going to play the scripture game with you. For every scripture you give me condemning money I will give you a scripture advocating money. Most of us use the Bible to further our own agendas or to justify our actions anyway. #TRUTH. Money can absolutely buy happiness.

My wife and I travel quite a bit. She just returned from a 7 day cruise. She was happy. We spent a week in NYC this spring. Our hotel was right in the heart of Times Square. We were happy. I'm currently on a plane, in first class, writing this chapter. I am happy. Last night while online I saw two shows that I want to take Erin to see. I spontaneously bout the tickets. I didn't have to wait till payday. She will definitely be happy. All these things take money. You see, my pastor Anthony McMillan teaches that happiness is determined by your circumstance. Happiness is derived from the root word happenstance. What money can't buy is JOY. Joy comes from within. My joy comes from my relationship with Christ. This joy that I have, the world didn't give it and the world can't take it away. That's what money can't buy. Yes, you can be broke and have joy at the same time... but why would you want to? I heard a quote a while back and I apologize that I can't remember who said it. The speaker stated that in order to achieve great things in life, no matter the area, we must ask ourselves three questions and then get to work.

Write these questions down and get to work.
Question #1: Where am I now?
Question #2: Where do I want to be?
Question #3: How do I get there?

Think about it. You can use this formula for any area of your life. Want a better marriage? Where am I now? Where do I want to be? How do I get there? Want a better job? Where am I now? Where do I want to be? How do I get there? These are the questions that I had to seriously ask myself in a few different areas of my life, especially our finances. We should continue to ask ourselves these three questions on a regular basis. Write them down, answer them truthfully and then get to work. Ask for help if you need it. But remember to seek help from an expert. You wouldn't ask a medical doctor how to rebuild a transmission, although the medical doctor is extremely smart. You would consult a certified mechanic because the mechanic is the expert. It's sad how many people take advice from unqualified individuals regarding finances. Is your mother an expert? How about your pastor? What about your spouse? These people may love you and care about you but please don't take financial advice from them unless their finances show them to be credible experts.

As a Christian, it absolutely bothers me when I see other Christians who are struggling and not living the life that God has planned for them. It's likely that they are excuse makers, just as I used to be. When you have more, you can do more and give more. Having money is not all about you. It's also about helping those around you. The people in Houston, TX have been hit hard with Hurricane Harvey. Facebook is covered with banners that read, "Pray for Texas". Yes, they need your prayers, but guess what they need just as much if not more than prayers? You guessed it…money. We sent money along with our prayers. The reason that most only sent prayers is because they didn't have the money to send. Some sent supplies, some went to help, and some took boats. All of those things cost money. We make jokes about not having the things we want in life to make ourselves feel better. Stop making jokes and stop making excuses.

FBFS Agency Manager Michelle Huburt invited me to the great state of Kansas this year to help train her agents. Kansas will always have a special place in my heart. It's where I got my start as a professional speaker. She showed a graph that read 69% of Americans have less than $1,000 in their savings account. Wow, that's a staggering and sad statistic. I believe it because I used to be in that 69% also. Why was I there? Excuses! If you're ready to move to the 8 out of 10 who don't live from paycheck to paycheck and the 31% who do have more than $1,000 in their savings, then keep reading.

Bill Gates, the richest man in America, remarked, "If you are born poor it's not your fault. But if you die poor it is your fault." Jack Ma, one of the richest men in all of Asia, remarked, "If you're still poor at age 35, then you deserve it." I bet that these statements would have most people angry. On the contrary, they motivate me to become better. In my opinion we live in the greatest country in the world. The opportunities we have in America are second to none. Obviously, we have our issues just like others but life can be superb for the person who's willing to go all out to make their dreams come true. Actor Will Smith remarked, "Set a goal so big that you can't achieve it until you grow into the person who can." I love it Will. Thank you sir.

A few years back I was doing some shopping for one of my daughter's birthday party. As I finished I headed to the check-out line. The line was long and there was only one cashier working. Being the talker that I am, I struck up a conversation with the gentleman behind me in line. When I discovered that he worked for Delta airlines I began to tell him that I always use Delta when I travel and how great they are. He began to tell me that the company wasn't great because it underpays their employees. He was a manager and earned a decent wage but the baggage handlers were earning a little over minimum wage. He believed that they should be paid more. When I asked why he felt the baggage handlers should be paid more he simply said, "Delta can afford it and it's not enough money." I asked, "What are their job duties?" As he began to give examples of their duties I inquired if he thought that it was a difficult job to learn? He agreed that it was not that difficult. Load bags on a plane and unload bags off a plane. It's a little more involved but that's the basics. I then asked, "If given some training do you believe that my teenage son could learn to do that job?" He agreed that he most likely could. I then asked, "If given some training did he think that my son could also fly the plane?" At his current age he agreed that it would be unlikely that he would be able to do so.

Here is the point I was making to him. We are paid according to the problem that we can solve. Solve a big problem you are paid more; Solve a small problem you are paid less. Loading and unloading bags is a small problem while flying a plane is a big problem and harder to solve. If you want to earn more money learn to solve bigger problems. So what problem are you solving?

OXYGEN

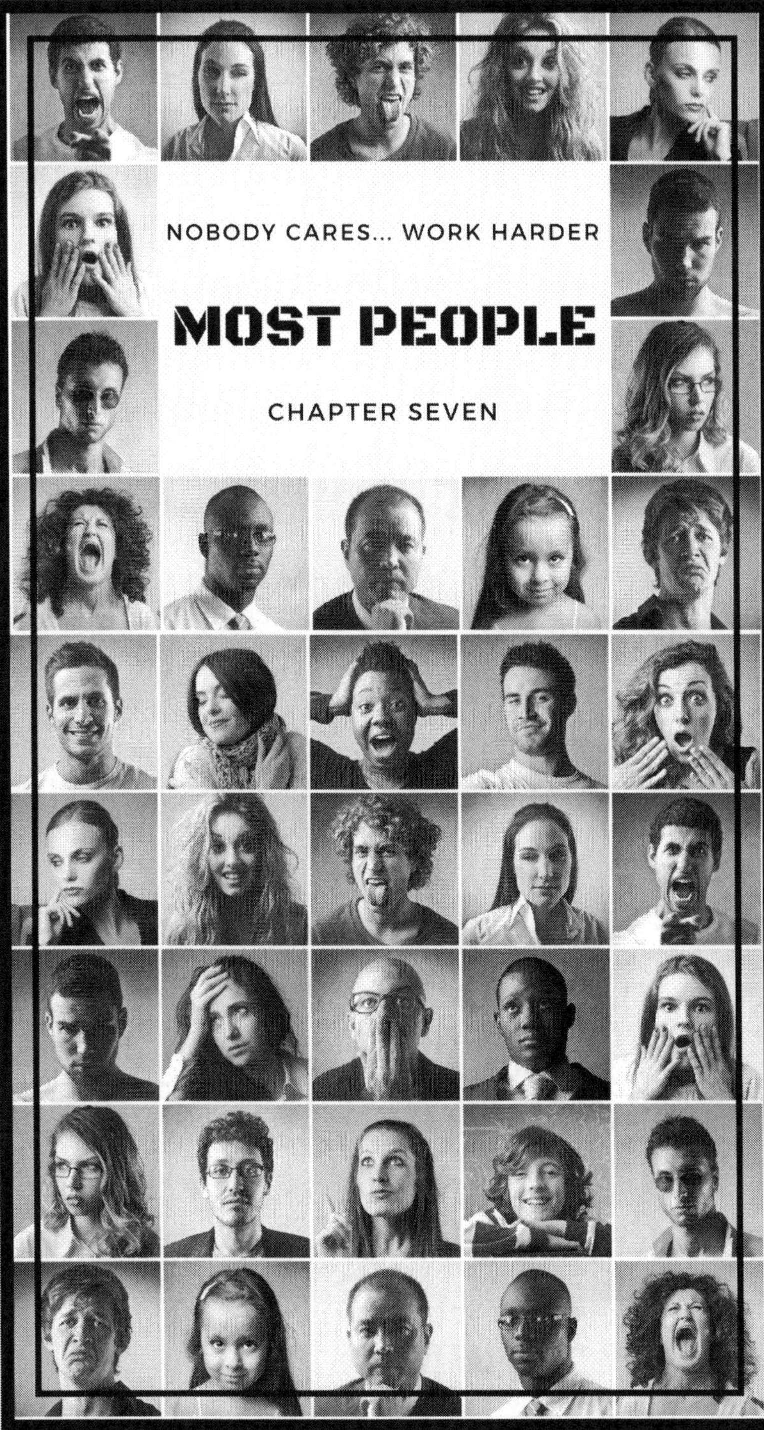
NOBODY CARES... WORK HARDER
MOST PEOPLE
CHAPTER SEVEN

MOST PEOPLE

I often travel the country teaching insurance agents and their teams how to sell more insurance policies. A big part of the training involves how to sell more life insurance. One of the best scripts used to start a life insurance conversation is, "Here's what most people tell me." The reason that this line works is because in our society most people want to do what others are doing. Most people follow the crowd. If this is what most people buy then I will buy it too. Everyone wants to believe that they are not a follower but the evidence against them is overwhelming. I bet that if you asked 100 people if they were a leader or a follower, 99 would say that they are a leader, but sadly their life would reveal just the opposite. Their life would reveal that they live a mediocre, no risks, very safe, excuse-riddled life. That's why most people receive what they do from life. Dr. Steve Maraboli observed, "The universe doesn't give you what you ask for with your thoughts; it gives you what you demand with actions." Most people dream of a better life but won't get off their butts and do what it takes to get what they want. Most people accept what life brings them rather than demanding from life what they want. Most people would have stayed at a guaranteed job while I chose the entrepreneur route.

I believe that God has given each of us a gift. Each of us has what it takes to succeed in this world. Notice that I didn't say survive. I said succeed or to thrive; To have what we want and desire in life. But again, most people have opted for the simple life. Not because it's what they desire, but because it's too hard to do anything else. While driving to the store one day my sixteen-year old son Judah asked, "Dad, does everyone in our family look up to you and mom because you are successful?" I told him that I wasn't sure. In fact, some people may actually be jealous of others who are successful. Personally, I love capitalism and I take every advantage of it that I can. Get out of my way and let me make as much money as I can. Keep your hourly wage and pay me my worth, my value that I bring to the table. Most people don't want that deal because most people don't bring much value to the table.

I asked Judah what he thought it took to be financially successful? He responded, "Hard work." I saw that this was a great teaching moment. I've been trying to instill words of wisdom in my boys, in addition to what they are learning in school. Ask them and they will tell you what Jim Rohn said about school, "Formal education will make you a living, while self-education will make you a fortune." Now ask any student, "Do you want to make a living or make a fortune?" I think you know the answer. Yet, most students only read books from school and most of them are fiction. But we don't live in a world of fiction now do we? As parents it's our job to prepare our children for the real world; the non-fiction world. Judah saw Erin and I cutting up our credit cards when the new ones arrived in the mail and asked why? At 16 he has a basic understanding of credit, credit scores & interest rates. Most sixteen year old's have no idea…quite frankly because their parents don't. Most people won't seek help from an expert in their finances. You wouldn't represent yourself in court or attempt to perform surgery on yourself, would you? Yet when it comes to finances and budgeting most people try to figure it out themselves.

Back to my conversation with Judah; I told him that hard work was only part of the equation. There are plenty of people who work hard but don't make a lot of money. They don't enjoy the finer things in life. They still live from paycheck to paycheck and struggle financially. The main reason is because they have made poor financial decisions in the past and are still paying for those decisions. What's worse is that most people still continue to make those same decisions that got them in to this predicament in the first place. Remember, I used to be most people in this area. If I can make the transition, you can as well. I told him that the money you earn is a direct reflection of the problem that you solve. We've already covered this. If you are working hard to solve an easy problem, then you will be compensated as such. Most people want to solve easy problems and that's why they struggle financially. Example: We know that sales is among the highest paid professions.

The sky is the limit for a great sales person. Yet, when you offer someone a sales position most people respond, "No thanks, I'm not a salesman." What they're really saying is, "That's too hard. I want something easier." As if everyone is born knowing exactly how to do what they are currently doing. It all takes training. It is a skillset that has to be developed. The easier the job the quicker the skillset is developed and the less money you make. The harder the job, the longer it takes to develop the skillset and the more money you make. It's really quite simple. I told Judah to choose his profession wisely. Although he already wants to be a speaker and join the network marketing profession which is one of the hardest professions to succeed in. So, what do you think his income will look like if he is successful? The sky is the limit. At sixteen Judah is already earning a residual income because he has shared samples of our product with other people. At the school's recent fundraiser, he was asked by an adult, "What would you like to do when you graduate?" Judah responded, "I'm going to be a speaker & network-marketer so I can earn residual income." He then had the courage to ask this adult if she knew what residual income was? She responded, "No." He began to explain that residual income is doing something one time but getting paid for it month after month, year after year. I was so proud. My lessons are sinking in. Most people choose to work harder than smarter. Imagine...the adult had never heard of residual income. Here's a quick lesson:

<u>LINEAR INCOME:</u> Work forty hours, get paid for forty hours. If you don't work, you don't get paid (Most People)
<u>RESIDUAL INCOME:</u> Sale something one time but you are paid a percentage of that sale each month as long as the person keeps paying their bill. Most sales people work on commission and start at zero each month. With residuals, you never start at zero. You are paid on what you have sold in the past. You can see how this starts to increase. Imagine earing a six-figure income based on what you did years ago. Multibillionaire Warren Buffet observed, "If you don't find a way to make money while you sleep, you will work until the day you die."
<u>LEVERAGED INCOME:</u> Being paid from the efforts

of others. Think about it. If the boss doesn't show up for work he/she still gets paid because you did show up for work. Remember that multibillionaire J. Paul Getty remarked, "I would rather make 1% on the efforts of 100 people than 100% on my own efforts."

When I left the insurance industry most agents questioned my decision. They couldn't understand why I would leave a some-what guaranteed successful business. And there is no doubt in my mind that I would have been an extremely successful insurance agent. But I have been doing the opposite of most people since age 37. That's when I began reading self-education books & listening to audio CD's and it has paid tremendous returns. In 2005 I walked away from the US Post Office to start my network marketing career with AmeriPlan. I earned more money & worked less hours. I looked forward to waking up every day and sharing my product. Most people are like the television show The Walking Dead. They are like zombies clocking in and out each day at a dead-end job that they hate...because it's easier than the alternative. They might as well be called the working dead. I left AmeriPlan and pursued my own insurance agency. It was the most money I'd ever made in my life; until now. I literally work less hours than I ever have and earn more than I ever have. How is that possible? Because now I solve bigger problems. I'm not telling you these things to brag. I'm letting you know that the financial dreams that you have for you and your family are absolutely possible. You must start thinking differently and doing things differently than you have in the past. Remember, your past decisions are the reason that you are where you are now. Get help from an expert and stop doing what most people do. It's actually pretty simple to be successful. All you have to do is the opposite of what most people do.

We see it in our everyday routine. Just look around you. Most people sleep in. Successful people rise early. Most people eat badly. Successful people eat healthy & exercise. Most people watch a lot of television. Successful people read self-education books. Most people live on linear income. Successful people have multiple streams of income. It's as simple as doing the opposite of most people. Just the other day I was riding with my daughters in the car. We pulled up to the light and the vehicle next to me was blasting their radio while the girls and I were listening to a self-education audio CD. I haven't listened to the radio in years. I watch the news maybe 2 or 3 times a year if it's related to weather or a national event. I just don't spend time on much stuff that's not MMA (money making activities) while most people do.

I have trained myself to think differently than most people. I often sit and think about how to earn more money and pay off debt at the same time. This is something that you can do as well. It takes calculated risk and like Judah said, "Hard work." Let's talk about risk for a quick second. Years ago, when we were struggling financially and barely paying the bills each month, I was presented with an opportunity to earn more money. We've all heard the saying, "No risk, no reward." We've also heard that it takes money to make money. Through my self-education I decided that if I wanted things to change in my life then I had to change them. Like Barry said, "No one was going to save me." I had to save myself." I was sick and tired of struggling like most people. The difference is that I was willing to do something about it when most people aren't. They whine and complain and wish that things were better. Or they blame someone else for their failures and lack of money, like the government or their boss.

I took a portion of our mortgage payment, invested in myself and went to work. That investment paid off and I haven't looked back since. When presented with the same opportunity I guarantee that most people would have said, "I don't have the money." You're right. And if you don't do anything different from what you're doing now you won't have the money next month either. In point of fact you'll be in the same situation this time next year and ten years from today. Remember the acronym for poor (Passing Over Opportunities Repeatedly). I made the decision that I refused to be in the same place this time next year. I got angry. I was downright pissed off and I was going to do something about it. I knew that God wanted better for me. I knew that he had better in store for me. I was determined to get everything that was mine; and yours too if you didn't go after it. (See Jeremiah 29:11) Author and speaker John Addison remarked, "I don't want my share. I want more than my share." I want more also. The best part is that you don't have to do anything immoral to receive more than your share. Most people leave their share on the table anyway. It's there for the taking.

Another reason that I succeed where most people fail is that I don't care what people think of me. I really don't. Now don't get me wrong. Everyone wants to be liked and I definitely want to have a stellar reputation. But your opinion of me means very little. Most people are held back because they are so worried about what others think of them. We've already covered this. Most people don't want to be embarrassed, so they play life very safe. I'm willing to take that risk and that is why I succeed. A friend of mine was offered a nice sum of money to speak at an event. The audience size was 30-40 people. He was familiar with the topic but was afraid that he would make mistakes and be embarrassed. He offered the job to me. I immediately accepted; and he knew the subject matter better than I did. I accepted because I don't mind being embarrassed. It's a learning opportunity. Dallas Mavericks owner Mark Cuban observed, "Perfection is the enemy of profitability." In *The 15 Laws of Invaluable Growth*, John Maxwell writes, "Growing can be a messy business. It means admitting you don't have the answers. It requires making mistakes. It can make you look foolish. Most people don't enjoy that. But that is the price of admission if you want to improve." So, I began studying for the event. I was nervous, but I still performed at my best. I made mistakes as well as having some good points. The audience liked what I had to say, and I also received a second speaking engagement from that one. I've done over 100 talks and 70% of them are by referrals. I'm not perfect. I continue to work on my craft.

Most people want it perfect before they say yes. They want everything in line before they step out. They have to pray about it first before they move forward.

And that is why most people do not succeed. Eric Worre says, "Say yes, tell the world, then figure it out." Most people try to figure it out first. In the Marines we had a battle cry. When we were about to get into action; When we were about to attack something, we would yell, "Get Some!" at the top of our lungs. Maybe you should have a battle cry. Maybe you should step outside your comfort zone right now and yell at the top of your lungs "Get Some." Or are you too embarrassed? It's okay if you don't. Most people won't anyway; and that's my point. Here's an exercise I do from time to time to prove my point of most people. I ask my audience, "If you want to be successful raise your hand." Inevitably everyone raises their hand. Then I ask, "If you want to be successful jump up and run around the room screaming I want to be successful." If I'm lucky, one person will move. Most people look at each other too embarrassed to move. That's why it's so easy to succeed in our society. There is no competition if you are willing to go the extra mile; If you're willing to look foolish. Most people dwell in the land of mediocrity. If you put forth just a little effort, you can outshine them all. I hate mediocrity. I know that hate is a strong word but that's exactly how I feel about it. I hate mediocrity. I especially hate it when I know that someone is playing beneath their capability and can be better; When they're not living up to their full potential and not using their God given abilities. Last week I had jury duty. It was my first time. I'd been called in the past but because of my law enforcement career and living out of state, I never had to serve. I arrived in the jury assembly room with 300 other prospective jurors. They lined us up like cattle, made us sit next to each other and watch a video about jury duty. Waiting to be called, it was extremely quiet in the room. 300 people and not one person said a word. I couldn't take it any longer. I stood up and said, "Hello everyone, my name is Steve, I'm a Scorpio and I enjoy long walks on the beach. Who's next?" Everyone began to laugh. Of course, no one else said anything but people did begin to talk with other. By the end of the day everyone including the clerks, bailiffs, lawyers and the judge knew juror #43 Mr. Wilmer. One of the other jurors remarked that I had a great attitude about jury duty. Once again, the only things you can control are your actions and your attitude. I ended up meeting and talking with a UPS pilot. We exchanged info and he is going to pass my info on for possible speaking engagements. Why? Because I'm not afraid to be embarrassed.

I attended a sales class in Oklahoma City. It was filled with top salesmen from California to New York. During the presentation the presenter asked, "Who's the best salesman in the room." Before I knew it, my mouth yelled, "I am." All eyes immediately fell on me. It was too late to take it back. I had to act "as if". When in doubt act as if you know what's going on. Always act the part. The presenter asked me to come to the front of the room and began role playing with me to see if I could get him to buy something from me. I eventually did, and I learned some valuable sales techniques along the way. I gained the respect of my peers and the presenter. He now has me speak 3-4 times a year during some of his presentations and he also has me training his staff on a monthly basis. Because I'm not afraid to be embarrassed I succeed where most people fail. Our society is full of most people; those who barely do the minimum to squeak by unnoticed. Those who are the working dead; Those who complain but aren't willing to do what it takes to succeed; Those who simply follow the crowd. As I said earlier, if you want to make a serious change in your life all you have to do is the opposite of what most people are doing. Now ask yourself…am I most people? And if you don't like your answer, it's never too late to change. Change starts in our mind. So, pick up a book, start there and I'll see you at the top… because the bottom is crowded... with MOST PEOPLE!

NOBODY CARES... WORK HARDER

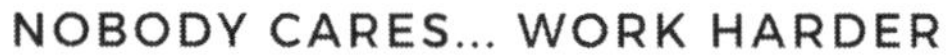

COW OR RHINO?

CHAPTER EIGHT

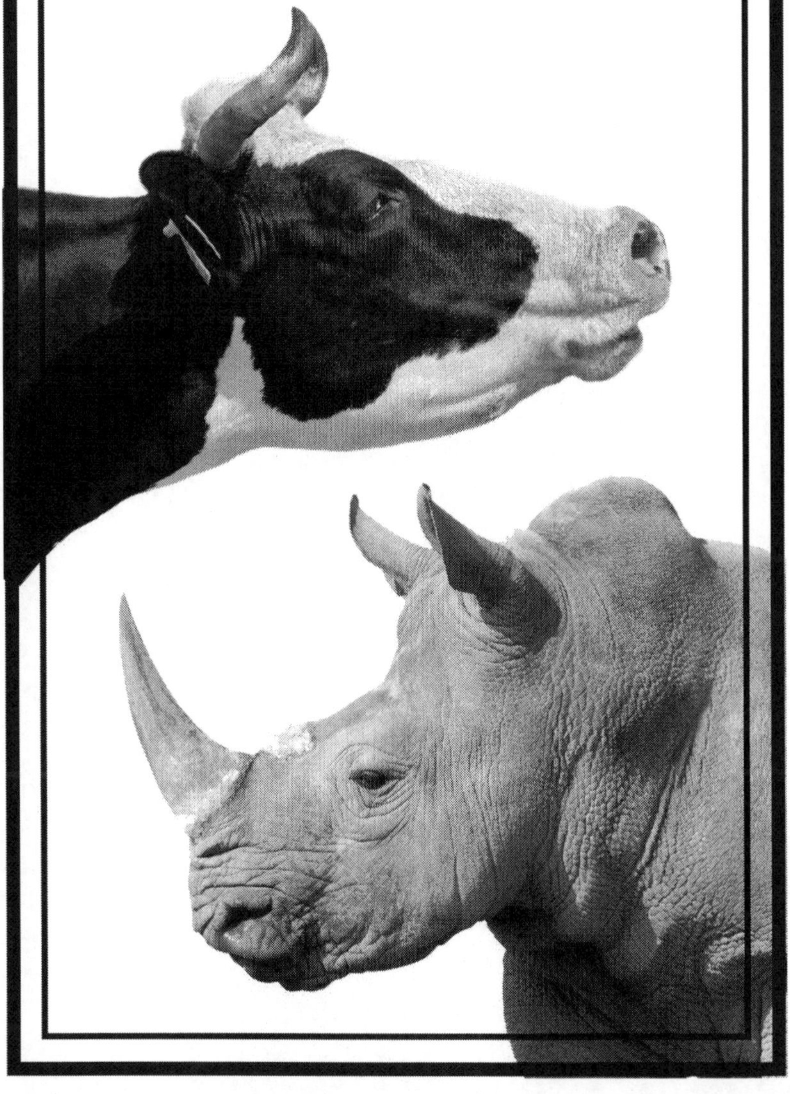

NOBODY CARES... WORK HARDER

COW OR RHINO?

I am always open to hearing about good books that people are reading; Good non-fiction self-education books of course. I want books that challenge me to become better and then gives me a plan or path to accomplish that mission. I was recently told about a book by the name of *Rhinoceros Success* written by Scott Alexander. I was told that the book was a good read, but the audio was even better. So, I downloaded the audio, gave it a listen…and I was not disappointed. In fact, I have listened to the audio at least three times over the last month. It speaks directly to me in ways that no other book has. It challenges me in ways that no other book has as well. If you like to be cuddled, cradled and handled with care, this book is not for you. But if you're like me, give it to me straight, rip the band-aid off, then you have got to take a listen. Put it in your car and listen to it as you drive around running errands. Keep a small recorder in your car or download a recording app on your phone. You will hear great things that you will want to record for later and then implement the lessons that you will learn. Garrison Wynn observed, "Knowledge is not power; Implementation of knowledge is power." In this chapter I will discuss some of the things that Scott Alexander addresses and give you my thoughts. Let me start by asking, "Are you a cow or are you a rhino?

Scott talks about success being deep in the jungle. It's not on the outskirts. It's not just around the corner. Cows are not willing to venture deep into the jungle. They know that there is danger deep in the jungle. Cows understand that they will not survive deep in the jungle. So, they stay in the safe zone, in the comfort zone, never going after success; never taking any chances. They are afraid of being eaten by bigger stronger animals. That's why you don't see cows in the jungle. A cow wouldn't last two seconds in the jungle. They are fat, lazy and content with laying around all day chewing their cud. They don't want success. They never think about success. When they do think about success it's only for a quick second. Then they quickly remember that they are a cow and go back to chewing, sleeping and grazing waiting to be slaughtered. There are cows around us every day. They don't want anything out of life. They are content in their current situation.

I say content because they won't attempt to do anything to change their situation. If you ask them, all cows say that they want a better life but their actions or should I say non-action tells a different story. If a cow gets the nerve to attempt something and fails, they quickly give up and head back to the pasture waiting to be slaughtered; Working at a job they hate for the next 50 years until they are unable to work anymore, only to hope that our government or family will take care of them.

A rhino doesn't sit around waiting. It charges after success until it finds it. And when it finds success, it loves it so much that it keeps charging looking for more. It doesn't give up if it fails once, twice, three times or more. A rhino is born in the jungle, so it knows that success is there somewhere. It just has to keep charging to find it. And you had not better get in the way of a charging rhino. It will run right over you or through you to obtain success. Not even the lion, the king of the jungle will get in the way of a charging rhino. I once witnessed an elephant get backed down by a rhino. It was a sight to see. Here's the point, rhinos charge on a daily basis looking for success. They don't let anything, or anyone get in their way. If they don't find success today or tomorrow you can best believe that they will keep charging until they do. They are willing to go deep. They are willing to take chances. They are willing to face obstacles, danger and even other rhinos to obtain success in all areas of life and business. A rhino has goals to accomplish. They know exactly what they want, and they are going after it. Even though a rhino may be afraid, they refuse to be intimidated by any other animal. They still charge in spite of their fear. Rhinos have a "eat or be eaten" mentality. You will not defeat a rhino without a fight. And if you defeat it, it will be a fight that you will not soon forget. I guarantee that you will have the battle scars to prove it. You will find the cow in the pasture not doing a single thing other than eating and "mooing" (complaining) waiting for the farmer to milk them and eventually be slaughtered. They have no goals and they don't want to fight for anything. Are you a cow or are you a rhino?

Rhinos associate with other rhinos. They are all charging together looking for success. They realize that that there is enough success for them all. They don't associate with other animals because other animals may not be on the same mission as they are. They surround themselves with other 6000lbs charging rhinos. They understand that this makes them better. It makes them stronger. They can learn different things from other rhinos. They learn how to hunt, how to survive, how to protect themselves and have more in life. A rhino is always trying to become better. If you're reading this book you are most likely a rhino or on your way to becoming one. I considered myself to be a rhino as well. But after reading Scott's book I realized that I still had some cow behaviors.

If you want to become a rhino you must stop associating with cows. You must find bigger rhinos to associate yourself with. A rhino's conversation is different than that of a cow. Rhinos don't mooooo (complain) all day long. A rhino looks for solutions to a problem rather than complain about the problem. A cow tells the leader about a problem and expects the leader to fix it. A rhino tells the leader about a problem and already has a solution to fix it. A mature rhino tells the leader about a problem and says that it's already fixed. Are you a Cow or a Rhino?

Cows will associate with any animal. They don't care. They associate with chickens, goats and pigs. No wonder they don't want anything out of life. Look who they're constantly surrounding themselves with. Chickens can't fly. They walk around all day flapping their wings, head down, eating crumbs from the ground, afraid of their own shadow. Think about the chickens in your life. They flap their wings saying what they're going to do but never do anything. They say where they want to go but never go anywhere. They are in the same place that they were in last year and the year before that and the year before that and the…you get the picture. They are afraid to take risks. They are afraid to try anything new. They live in their chicken coop (comfort zone) also waiting to end up on the dinner table. A chicken coop is full of crap everywhere you look. That's because chickens constantly crap on you. They want to keep you down on the ground with them. So, they will crap all over you, your ambitions, and your dreams. They don't want you to be a rhino.

A goat will eat anything in sight. They don't care what it is. Goats are always grumpy and in a bad mood. Who do you know that's always watching television? Who is always on social media? They eat anything. They let all kinds of junk into the minds. They can tell you all about the latest television shows this fall but haven't picked up a book since high school. They're always in a bad mood because they hate their life and they want you to hate yours as well.

A pig rolls around all day in slop and doesn't care what it looks like. It's a pig because it doesn't care about what it puts in its mouth. It's a pig because it doesn't care about its appearance. A pig is absolutely fine with how it looks and it's not willing to do anything to change its appearance. It also will eventually end up on the breakfast table & dinner table. Wow, these are the animals that a cow surrounds himself with. No wonder a cow doesn't want anything out of life. None of his friends want anything out of life either. They aren't going to challenge the cow to become better. They won't say anything to the cow at all. They don't want the cow to leave the pasture. We're all going to die soon anyway so let's all die together. A rhino would never be associated with these animals. Are you a cow or are you a rhino?

A rhino has two-inch-thick skin. It's difficult to hurt a rhino. You had better have an extremely sharp object or an extremely powerful gun to take down a rhino. By the same token, if you're a rhino you must have thick skin as well. Rhinos don't let what people say to them get them down. Most rhinos use negativity as fuel. Tell a rhino that they can't accomplish a goal and they will likely charge right over you…if it's a goal that they want to accomplish in the first place. Remember, your words don't mean much to a rhino. In Marine Corps boot camp my drill instructors didn't motivate us by telling us that we could do it. They told us that we couldn't do it and said that we should just give up and go home. They were looking for rhinos. They were separating us from the cows. I was a cow my first two weeks into boot camp. I was held back for having a cow attitude.

I spent fifteen weeks at Parris Island, SC while most of my rhino buddies graduated two weeks ahead of me. I finally got it together and transformed myself into a hard-charging rhino. So, the good news is that even if you are a cow at this point in your life, it's not too late to make the shift to a full-fledge 6000lbs charging rhino. Develop a thick skin. Most criticism comes from cows anyway, and a rhino doesn't care what a cow has to say. They keep charging. If you are in sales you definitely must develop a thick skin. You're going to hear the word no far more time times than you will hear the word yes. A rhino understands that it's a numbers game. How many no's can you stomach to get to your yes? Do you have the thick skin that it takes? The rhino understands that "no" only means not right now. The rhino understands that 80% of sales are made on the 5th-12th contact so they keep charging. A rhino will never stop until the task is completed, and then they're off charging towards the next goal.

A cow on the other hand has thin skin. It's easily

hurt, wounded or even killed. You can kill a cow with your words. Tell a cow it can't be done, and they will give up and go home. Tell a cow it's never been done before, and they will agree quickly and give in. Tell a cow it's hard, and they will return to the pasture to chew their cud and wait for the day to be slaughtered. A cow never follows up with a prospect. A cow won't contact a prospect more than twice. A cow gives up when a prospect says no. Remember the best sales book ever written? It was written by a famous doctor. Dr. Seuss wrote *Green Eggs and Ham*. Sam-I-Am was a rhino. He was a charging rhino. Every time his prospect said no, he kept charging asking more questions until finally he made the sale. I have an insurance background and my success came because I was a rhino. I wasn't always a rhino, but I developed my skillset over the years. I now train others all across the country in the art of insurance sales. Here's what I have noticed over the years in this industry. Most insurance producers are cows.

Ouch, I know that hurts, but rhinos tell you the truth because they want you to become better. Rhinos want you to succeed. If I were a cow I would tell you that you're doing a great job and you shouldn't change a thing. I want you to become a rhino. I train teams on exactly what to say, what not to say and how to say it.

Rhinos will implement the training, cows won't. Cows return to the pasture…you know the rest. Note that I said earlier that I developed my skillset. Rhinos are willing to put in extra work to become better. Cows aren't. Rhinos will practice on their own time. Cows won't. Rhinos will spend their own money on classes, seminars, books, training, etc. Cows won't. Subsequently, rhinos will make more money, qualify for trips, grow their business & have more fun. Cows won't. Are you a cow or are you a rhino?

Rhinos are open to the next opportunity. Rhinos take calculated risks. They are willing to lose a little for a chance to win big. They understand that money is a tool. If the tool is used correctly it will reproduce after its own kind. There is risk in investments. But invest wisely and you have your money work for you rather than you working for your money. There are business opportunities around us every day. A rhino seeks to earn more because they understand that when you have more you can do more. A rhino doesn't let a little thing like "lack of money" stop them. They research, get a loan, get a grant, borrow from a friend, sweat equity, etc. Rhinos do whatever it takes. They look for ways to get it done rather say why it can't be done.

What did Henry Ford say? "Whether you think you can or you can't, you're right." He was a big rhino. A rhino is never satisfied with their performance. It can always be better. Gloria Steinem somewhat remarked, "Rhinos plan for three generations. Cows plan for Saturday night." My wife and I are building generational wealth. Cows go to their jobs every day and only think of the weekend. Thank God it's Friday. Again, there is nothing wrong with having a job…that you love…that you perform well. You can be a rhino at your job. But always remain open to other opportunities. Rhinos will always have multiple streams of income. Their livelihood will never be based on one source. Cows only believe in having once source. And what happens when a cow breaks its leg? It doesn't produce anymore so it's taken out back and shot. How many times have you seen someone lose their job or business and their entire world is turned upside down? It's because their world was being held together with duct tape, chewing gum and paper clips, one paycheck away from bankruptcy. How did this happen; Passing Over Opportunities Repeatedly. Remember my Uber story? I was thinking like a cow. Remember the cell phone story? He was thinking like a cow. It's hard to hear opportunity knocking when you're too busy knocking the opportunity. Be open to opportunities that come your way. Are you a cow or are you a rhino?

Rhinos have self-discipline. One of the best definitions of discipline I have ever heard came from my wife Erin. She observed, “Discipline is simply choosing between what you want now and what you want most.” Rhinos choose what they want most. If a rhino has a certain goal they don’t allow temptations to win. They remain focused on the task at hand. Erin and I are currently on a mission to become completely debt free. She wants a house on the beach so of course I’m going to make that happen for her. That’s what rhinos do. We both understand that there are certain luxuries that we must forfeit for the time being to have what we want most, not what we want now. Every time we make a sacrifice we say, “Do what we must do now, so we can do what we want to do later.” Cows don’t understand this principle. If a cow wants something they go out and get it. Cows don’t consider the cost. They are run by their emotions, never making wise decisions.

I was a cow when I bought that new Lexus. I didn’t consider the cost and it nearly broke me. Cows live in the here & now rarely planning for the future. Rhinos stay rich by living like they’re broke. Cows stay broke by living like they’re rich. I had a sign on my wall in huge black letters. It was meant for every customer to read when they sat down at my desk. It read, "There are two pains in life. The pain of discipline and the pain of regret." Discipline weighs ounces while regret weighs tons. Disciplining others is easy. Rhinos have self-discipline. Rhinos eat chicken breast while cows are eating fat burgers. Rhinos practice their craft while cows are on social media. Rhinos exercise while cows are still sleeping. Rhinos read books while cows are watching television. No one is making rhinos do these things. Rhinos do these things because they understand that it makes them better. Rhinos understand sacrifice. Maxwell Maltz observed, "The ability to discipline yourself to delay gratification in the short term in order to enjoy greater rewards in the long term is the indispensable prerequisite for success." Are you a cow or a rhino?

Just because your parents were a cow doesn't mean that you have to be one. Just because your parents were a rhino doesn't guarantee that you will be one. Generational wealth can start with you if you're willing to make the transition from cow to rhino. My wife and I are making that transition. This transition will affect our children as well. Erin and I were talking about the success that we're having in our business. We will be in a better position to help our children so that they don't struggle the way we did. Rhinos understand that it's not just about them. It's about building a legacy. Rhinos leave an inheritance for their children's children. When you obtain more you can do more for others. I recently taught about finances at my church. I made reference to Scott's book from the pulpit. Yes, there are rhinos and cows in church as well. A good starting point to make your transition is by reading *The Richest Man in Babylon* by George S. Clason. It's an easy but good read. It gives you seven remedies for a lean purse. Did I mention that I'm on my way to becoming a millionaire? I believe that I did. It's really not that hard. Scott Alexander remarked, "There are books written by rhinos that tell you exactly what to do to become wealthy. Cows won't read them…and they can read." They are in the pasture chewing their cud, associating with chickens, goats and pigs, complaining about everything waiting to be taken to slaughter. A rhino decides to charge after success. It doesn't matter to a rhino if no one befor them experienced success. A rhino doesn't mind being first. They lead the way for other baby rhinos. Are you a cow or are you a rhino?

I could go on and on giving examples of the differences between rhinos and cows. But I don't have that type of time. I'm a rhino and I have rhino things to do and goals to accomplish. Basically, we all get to decide if we are to be a cow or rhino. If you don't like being a cow, then change it. Get help from a rhino. Ask a rhino what must you do to become a rhino as well. Rhinos are always willing to help. We won't do it for you, but we will lend a helping hand. Trust me. Rhinos don't get asked for help too often. Most cows don't want help. They enjoy the pasture. It's nice and comfortable there. Think about this, when I am training my clients most are not proficient in sales, with a few exceptions. They all have my personal cell phone. I constantly tell them to call me with questions or concerns. Call me if you can't handle an objection. Call me if you don't know what to do. Here's a shocker…very few ever call me. I only hear from the rhinos. Where are the cows? You guessed it…in the pasture chewing that delicious cud.

Stephen Luke observed, "You are the CEO of your own life. Start making executive decisions today." Decide if you want to continue on the path that you are currently on. Ask yourself where you will be in a year from now if you don't make a decision to change. It all starts with a decision. Our lives are shaped by our decisions. And just to be clear, no decision is also a decision.

One of my favorite scriptures in the bible is found in Deuteronomy 30:19. It reads, "This day I call heaven and earth as witnesses against you. I have set before you, life and death, blessings and curses. Now choose life that you and your children may live." You must decide if you want life. You must decide if you want blessings. Then you must get up and start working towards what you want. No one else knows what you want. And no one else will be as disappointed as you if you don't get it. Rhinos make the tough decision because they know what must be done. Sometimes the toughest thing and the right thing are the same thing. Cows don't make decisions. They let other people make decisions for them. They let others dictate their lives. You decide, "Yes or no, in or out, up or down, live or die, fight or give in, rhino or cow, you decide. So, make your decision now. Are you a cow or are you a rhino?

WORDS

CHAPTER NINE

health
creativity
passionate
work intelligence job
goals positive
mindset
mind leader technology
strategy solutions
plan
communicationcareer
dream teamwork
forward achievement
challenge inspiring
comfort
future philosophy
Take Action
business ideas
confidence
solution
innovation think
growth creative inspiration
education
vision wisdom
motivational
idea ambition success
wealthy energy
planning big
ahead

NOBODY CARES... WORK HARDER

WORDS

<u>FEAR</u>: Ralph Waldo Emerson remarked, "What you are afraid to do is a clear indication of what you need to do." Now I am not in the habit of telling people what they need to do. Most people don't listen anyway. We are all afraid of something. There is no such thing as being fearless. The difference is that the winners in this world don't allow fear to stop them from doing what's necessary to succeed. We are not afraid to do the easy things. It's the difficult things that we fear. It's the change that we fear. It's the unknown that frightens us. Most are okay with staying in their comfort zone. It's the things that frighten us that makes us stronger when we move pass fear. I did not say that we conquer fear. We move pass it because although we are afraid we get the job done. We must take risks if we are going to have a fulfilling life. Nothing great happens playing it safe. The next time that you are afraid to do something, you should probably do it. Step out on faith. Put your faith to work (Action).

In the Bible, James said that faith without works is dead. Fear has two meanings. Forget everything and run or face everything and rise. The choice is yours. But know this: If you run, you will most likely be running for the rest of your life. Face your fears and get the job done. Once you do, you will realize that it's nowhere near as bad as you thought that it was. Les Brown observed, "Too many of us are not living our dreams because we're too busy living our fears." Are you living your fears? Are you more worried about what could go wrong rather than what could go right? Don't fear failure. Fear being in the exact same place this time next year. Fear makes us stand still or often times take a step back.

One of my favorite actors is Richard Gere. He played in a movie called *First Knight*. It centered around King Arthur, Lancelot and the knights of the round table. In one scene Gere (Lancelot) was attempting to circumnavigate a dangerous gauntlet that all others previously failed. After completing the gauntlet rather easily, King Arthur asked, "How did you succeed where all others failed?" Lancelot replied, "Perhaps fear made them go back when they should have gone forward." What is fear keeping you from doing? Are you stepping backwards when you should be moving forward? Then maybe that's why you're in the same place, same spot, same situation that you've been in for years. And you'll remain there if you don't do something differently. Don't allow fear to hold you hostage. Don't allow fear to steal your dreams.

THOUGHTS: I absolutely believe that your thoughts are important. Most of the battle is in our mind. But Dr. Steve Maraboli remarked, "The universe doesn't give you what you ask for with your thoughts. It gives you what you demand with your actions." How many times have you been thinking about losing weight but haven't done it? You've been thinking about quitting that job and starting your business, but you haven't done it. This book started in my thoughts, but it wouldn't have been written if I didn't put action behind my thoughts. Everything we do, every great thing that we accomplish starts in that brain of ours. It starts with a thought. So, beware of stinking thinking. Don't let your thoughts talk you out of a great idea.

Your thoughts have a huge role to play in your success or failure. While we're on the subject, remember that failure is not the opposite of success, it's part of it. For years I thought that I couldn't write a book, so I didn't. I changed my thoughts and now I've written three over the last two years and I will start on my fourth in a few months. Thoughts have power. You have the ability to make your world or break your world by how you consistently think. So, control your thoughts. Don't let your thoughts control you.

<u>POTENTIAL</u>: "He has great potential." That's all fine and well but what is he doing with all that potential? The word potential is always used as a compliment. But if we look closer at the word it's really saying that you haven't done anything yet. It's possible that you could do it but as for now you haven't done a thing. Don't we all have potential? Didn't God give us all potential? Joyce Meyer observed, "Potential is like a priceless treasure, like gold. We all have hidden treasures within, but we have to dig to get it out." So why aren't more people living up to their potential? It's quite simple actually. Most people aren't willing to dig to get it out. They aren't willing to put in the work to unlock their potential. So, it stays on the inside of them, never sharing their gift with the world. Albert Schweitzer remarked, "The tragedy of life is what dies inside a man while he still lives." Make sure that your dream, your gift, your potential doesn't die inside of you. Share it with the world. Steve Wilmer (yes I'm speaking in third person) observed, "Your gift is not for you. It's for those around you. It will reward you but it's not for you." Think on this. There is no heavier burden than unfulfilled potential. Do not let this statement

relate to you.

<u>ASSOCIATION</u>: Show me your friends and I'll show you your future. That's a very powerful and true statement whether you like it or not; whether you agree with it or not. The fact remains that successful people tend to associate with other successful people. Middle-class Americans associate with other middle-class Americans. Poor people associate with other poor people. Criminals associate with other criminals and so on and so forth. It's because we feel comfortable being around people who are like us. But there is danger in the comfort zone. Nothing grows or becomes better in the comfort zone.

We should always strive to become better in each area of our lives; Therefore, we should associate ourselves with those individuals who can help us in those areas. If you can't change the people around you, you must change the people around you. Let that sink in for a minute. If you're the smartest person in the room, find a new room. You will never grow unless you challenge yourself. It feels good being the authority but never quit learning. Did you know that you become like the five people you spend the most time with? Were you also aware that your income is the average of those five people? Take a second and think about those five. If you want to grow, change your starting five. If you want your income to grow, change your starting five. Surround yourself with people that reflect who you want to be. Proverbs 27:17 reads, "Iron sharpens iron, so a man sharpens the countenance of his friend." Fate chooses our relatives, we choose our friends, so choose wisely.

ACTION: My mother would often say to me, "Wilmer, don't talk about it. Be about it." She was basically telling me that talk is cheap. It takes action to get things done. Talking only slows things down. Don't talk, act. Don't say, show. Don't promise, prove. It absolutely irks me (is that a word?) to hear people talk who don't act. We all know that person that is going to do this and that and then some. That person who is going to change their circumstances. That person who is going to write the book, start that business, get a better job, change their life, etc. but they never do a darn thing. Action speaks louder than words. You are what you do, not what you say you'll do. We must remember that action is the foundational key to all success.

Success in any area does not happen without action. Action proves who you are. Words only prove who you want to be. So, who are you? Here is the quote on all of my marketing material, "The distance between dreams & reality is called action." Everyone has dreams, although most have given up on theirs. The problem with dreams is reality. You can dream about a better life, a better this or that, but the reality is that until you take action, nothing will ever change. Do you have a James in your life? Remember what he said? Faith (belief) without works (action) is dead. You can believe all you want, but if you have no action to accompany your belief you're wasting your time. Dale Carnegie observed, "Inaction breeds fear. Action breeds confidence and courage." If you want to conquer fear, do not sit home and think about it. Go out and get busy." Are you breeding fear or courage in your life? Also remember that courage is not the absence of fear. Courage means that you take action although you are afraid. You move in spite of your fear. So, take action on whatever it is that you have been afraid to do, whatever it is that you have been thinking about doing.

> "Strength doesn't come from what you can do. It comes from overcoming the things you once thought you couldn't"

PROCRASTINATION: No such thing. It's either a priority to you or it's not. Enough said.

GIVING: This is an important attribute that is often overlooked. The world calls it karma. What you do will return to you. The bible calls it sowing and reaping. Galatians 6:7 says, "Whatsoever a man sows (does) that shall he also reap (receive). If you give money you will receive money. If you give friendship you will receive friendship. If you want to be blessed financially you must give. If you are a Christian you must give tithes and offering. Pastor Anthony McMillan observed that the first rule of money is that it's not yours to begin with. God gave you the ability to get wealth so 10% should go back to him first. Give your time to others. Never become too busy to help others. Volunteer your time. Your greatness is not what you have. It's what you give. Never get caught up in things. Never get lost in your possessions. Mark 8:36 says, "What does it profit a man to gain the whole world yet forfeit his soul?" So, what are you holding on to and what are you giving to others?

Winston Churchill observed, "We make a living by what we get. We make a life by what we give." Luke 6:38 reads, "Give and it shall come back to you. Good measure, pressed down, shaken together and running over shall men give to you." Once again you reap what you sow. Are you sowing? Are you planting to receive a harvest? I give constantly to others. I sporadically give to strangers. I drop money on the ground in airports and stores. I often pay for stranger's meals at restaurants. I constantly give God's money to others and that is a large part of why I am blessed financially. Doors just seem to open for me. People contact me all the time wanting to give me business. God sends me business, I make money, I give tithes & offering, I give to others, God sends me more business, I make money, I give tithes & offering, I give to others, God sends me more business…and so on. It's a never-ending cycle. Can God trust you with his money? Will you be faithful, or will you rob God? Malachi 3:8 says, "Will a man rob God? Yet you rob me. How do we rob you? In tithes and offering." I dare you to start giving. See what happens when you open your hands to others. God will surely bless you.

<u>SKILLSET:</u> People are always complimenting me when I train them in sales. They literally say it's the best training they've ever attended. I am flattered, but I'm quick to tell them that my success comes from skill, not talent. Skill means that you are able to do something well. When they took Liam Neesom's daughter in the movie Taken, he said, "I have a very particular set of skills. Skills that I have acquired over a very long ca-

reer. Skills that make me a nightmare for people like you." I am able to do what I do extremely well because I constantly work on my skillset. It's not talent...it's skills. Because it's skills, it means that anyone can learn to do what I do if they're willing to put in the work. I wasn't born with this ability, it was developed. I practiced over and over while others took time off. Now my skillset allows me to make a very good living. From the projects to the podium to seven figures. Ain't God Good? Ervin, don't you dare correct that statement! Are you working on your skills or are you done when five o'clock arrives? I'm working on my skills when I'm driving my kids around. It's 11:16pm and I'm writing while others are sleeping or watching television. I'm doing MMA (Money-Making Activities). What are you doing? My buddy Tony Robbins preaches that repetition is the mother of skills. My friend Mitchell Price remarked, "Do it again and again and again, not until you get it right, but until you can't get it wrong." My good friend Jim Rohn said that you must either modify your dreams or magnify your skills. Pat Falvey commented, "Skills are freedom, so get skilled up." When you have a particular set of skills, people will pay handsomely for you to use those skills. People will come from miles around to witness those skills. I love the Lionel Messi quote, "It took me 17 years and 114 days to become an overnight success."

That's skill ladies and gentlemen. How long have you been developing your skillset? Yea…it shows!

<u>LEADERSHIP:</u> When I talk to a boss I get the feeling that they are important. When I talk to a leader I get the feeling that I am important. That should be all that I have to say about leadership. That statement sums it up don't you think? Are you a leader or a boss? Really? What do your employees say? What does your family say? Do you lead from the front by example or push people around from the back? Do you say go or let's go? No one likes working for a boss (double s.o.b spelled backwards). We all want to follow a leader. Dr. John Maxwell observed, "A leader is someone who knows the way, goes the way and shows the way." A leader does it all. In order to become a great leader, you must first become a great follower. Although you may know more than your leader or be more experienced than your leader, your job as a follower is to line up with their vision. If you speak negative, people will do the same to you if you're ever given that position. You will reap what you sow.

A leader does what's right, not what's easy. A good leader listens to their people and then makes wise decisions. Andy Stanley pronounced, "Leaders who don't listen will soon be surrounded by people who have nothing to say." That's a lonely state. Dr. Maxwell also said that leaders become great not because of their power, but because of their ability to empower others. Who are you empowering? Who are you leading? More importantly, who's following you? If no one is following you then you are not a leader. You're simply on a long walk. Coach Vince Lombardi observed, "Leaders aren't born, they're made. And they're made just like anything else…through hard work."

ATTITUDE: Life is 10% of what happens to you and 90% of how you respond to it. Joyce Meyer mentioned, "A positive attitude gives you power over your circumstances rather than your circumstances having power of you." Bad things happen to us all. Some worst than others. I'm not saying that it's going to be easy to have a good attitude, but I can tell you that having a good attitude makes you feel better. A good attitude can often change the situation as well. The truth is that people see your attitude in the midst of your situation and make a determination whether or not they want to help you. A good attitude goes a long way. I was just sharing with my son this morning how a bad attitude overshadows your accomplishments. No one wants to be associated with a talented superstar who has a bad attitude.

It's poison. Your attitude determines your altitude. The better your attitude the higher you climb. A negative attitude will never give you a positive life. I choose to have a good attitude. I choose to look on the bright side. Once again, I'm not saying that it's easy. I constantly struggle to watch my attitude because I'm so critical of others and myself. If things aren't done correctly I can easily become upset if I allow myself to focus on the negative rather than the positive. Take a deep breath, smile & respond rather than reacting to the situation. Remember, the only two things you have control over in this life are your actions and your attitude. A bad attitude is like a flat tire. You can't get very far unless you change it. Make a choice to have a positive attitude. And by chance if you encounter one of those people who choose to be negative, that does not give you permission to respond in-kind. Let your smile change the world. Don't let the world change your smile.

<u>PURPOSE</u>: Bishop TD Jakes commented, "If you can't figure out your purpose, figure out your passion. For your passion will lead you right into your purpose." We were all put here on earth for a reason. It's not just happenstance that we're here. God doesn't do anything without a purpose. Unfortunately, most people simply go through life without ever discovering their purpose.

Do you know your purpose? Do you know why you're here? My wife says that my purpose is to preach Jesus and draw the lost to him. I agree. My purpose is market-place ministry; the business world. I have the anointing of the evangelist. I speak, and people listen. I know my purpose so I'm working my purpose. I figured it out because it's also my passion to speak and encourage others. Turn your passion into your paycheck and you'll never work another day in your life. Mark Twain observed, "The two most important days in your life are the day that you were born and the day you realize why." This is one of my favorite quotes. There is a genuine sense or fulfillment when you understand why you were put here on earth. You look forward to waking up every day to fulfill that purpose. Allow your passion to become your purpose and it will one day become your profession. You see, the most successful people in this world follow their passion, not paychecks. What are you following?

CHARACTER: H. Jackson Brown, Jr. declared, "Our character is what we do when we think no one is looking." What do you do when you think no one is looking? Most like to think that they are a person of good character. We all have people in our lives who have proven otherwise. Good character doesn't steal time from their employer by showing up late, leaving early and spending company time on social media. Good character doesn't say that they did their best when they know that they could've pushed a little harder to help that customer, make the extra calls or make that sale. Good character takes responsibility when they didn't get the job done and doesn't blame others. Yes, these things reflect your character. And if you really want to reveal someone's true character simply apply pressure. We should be more concerned about our character instead of our reputation. Our character is who we really are. Our reputation is who others think we are. We can all fake it in public. We all have a public perception. But what is our character at home? What does our family have to say? Our reputation means absolutely nothing to them. They see us for who we truly are. We should live in such a way that if someone spoke badly of us no one would believe it. I heard about an employer who met his prospective employees at a restaurant. He paid the server extra money to deliberately botch the order and get everything wrong to see how the prospect would respond. He was testing their character. If they passed the test he would invite them to the office for a second interview. He made sure that there was crumpled up paper on the floor in the waiting room. If they picked it up, they passed the second test; If not, they weren't hired.

Both of these examples give you an indication of a person's character. Michael Josephson observed, "People of character do the right thing even if no one else does, not because they think it will change the world but because they refuse to be changed by the world." And my good friend Mahatma Ghandi stated, "We must become the change we wish to see in the world." It's all about a person's character. So, what do you do when you think no one is watching?

GRATITUDE: I would often ask my customers to tell me something that they are grateful for? I wanted them to focus on the positive rather than the negative. It's impossible to be upset and grateful at the same time. When I find myself becoming frustrated because something didn't go as I'd planned, I think about the things I'm grateful for. I doubt that most people ever take the time to be grateful for anything. Most believe that they are entitled vs. being grateful. Someone once said that we should even be grateful for the bad things that happen in life. They open our eyes to all the good things that we weren't paying attention to before. There's an old saying that goes, "I used to complain about not having any shoes until I met a man with no feet." We all think we have it so bad. My kids have no idea how good they have it compared to my childhood. And that's the way

I want it. I don't want them to struggle as I did. But I'm trying to teach them to be grateful for what they have. As adults we can be extremely ungrateful as well. Tony Robbins told a story where people on an airplane were yelling and cursing because the wi-fi went down. Forget the fact that they were actually flying through the air, eating and drinking cold beverages. Forget the fact they would arrive at their destination within hours where as in the past it would have taken days. The smallest things tend to frustrate us rather than be grateful…because we feel entitled. We've become too comfortable. As you waste your breath complaining about what you don't have, remember that there is someone right now taking their last breath. Be grateful. I am blessed with everything I need. I am working hard towards everything I want. And most of all, I am grateful to God for what I have.

GOD: I was always told that you save the best for last. So, what better way to end this? He is the great I AM, the beginning and the end. He is my provider, my refuge, my strength, my Lord. Although I miss the mark often, I strive to please him every day. True peace comes from knowing that God is ultimately in control. Whatever you may be going through or dealing with, I urge you to seek God. I urge you to talk to him. He asks that you cast all your cares and worries on him because he cares for you. His book is filled with promises that he has for you. Yes you. It doesn't even matter if it's been a while since you've talked to him or if you've never talked to him. He is still waiting for you like a loving father waiting for his child to return home. He can hardly stand it he's so excited. He is ever present. He's not this untouchable being in the sky that you can't reach. Prayer is nothing more than talking to him. You don't have to shout, you don't have to be on bended knee and your words don't have to be elegant. He will still hear you. And I'm telling you that God still answers prayers. He loves us. Romans 8:38 reads, "For I am convinced that neither death nor life, neither angels nor demons, neither the present nor the future, nor any powers, neither height nor depth, nor anything in all creation will be able to separate us from the love of God that is in Christ Jesus our Lord." He loves us so much that he wanted to make sure to mention everything so that there was no room for doubt.

Sometimes I see people on the street corners yelling to repent. They are right. We must repent and turn away from our sins, lest we end up in the fiery lake meant for the devil and his angels. But it's the love of God that going to get people to seek him. It's the love of God that's going to save us, that's going to save the world. Yep, I am convinced that God loves me. And you should be assured…that he's especially fond of you too.

NOBODY CARES... WORK HARDER

CONCLUSION

NOBODY CARES... WORK HARDER

CONCLUSION

So, there you have it my friends. At least I hope we're still friends. I know that this may have been a tough read for some of you. Trust me, it was tough writing it because I was challenged at every turn. The message is always for the author first and the reader second. In the introduction I said that *Nobody Cares, Work Harder* was written by the Holy Spirit. God is looking for us to be strong soldiers (Marines) in his army. We can't do that if we have a defeated mindset. We can't go into the enemy's camp and take back the things he has stolen from us with a wimpy attitude and demeanor.

In Matthew 11:12 (KJV) Jesus said, "And from the days of John the Baptist until now, the Kingdom of Heaven suffereth violence, and the violent take it by force." We must become good foot soldiers for God. We must be strong and mighty in the Lord and ourselves. We have been assured by God's word that we are more than a conqueror and that we can do all things through Christ who gives us strength. Use that strength to further the Kingdom. Model your life after Christ. Yep, Jesus was most definitely a rhino. Matthew 5:48 read's,

"Be therefore perfect, even as your Father which is in Heaven is perfect." And we are made perfect, not in our own strength, but through Christ the great redeemer.

Know that this book was written in love (tough love) to challenge you to become the very best version of you that you can be. God bless you, and remember, Nobody Cares, Work Harder.

STEVE SPEAKS

NOBODY CARES... WORK HARDER

NOBODY CARES... WORK HARDER

NO PLAN B

BONUS CHAPTER BY ERIN WILMER

NOBODY CARES... WORK HARDER

NO PLAN B

BY ERIN L. WILMER

It was nearly six years ago. I'd just retired from twenty-four years of honorable service in the United States Navy. Now here I was, sitting in a small class room with twelve others in St Louis, Missouri. I was a young unlicensed broker with Edward Jones Investments. I was insecure, a bit frightened, and a little nervous, just to name a few of the emotions I was feeling at the time. I hadn't felt this way since I was a young sailor in boot camp. As the Chief, I made others feel nervous, now the shoe was on the other foot. I'd just spent the last eight weeks vigorously studying for the Series 7 Securities Exam. This exam was a federal requirement to become a financial advisor. It was pass or fail, but for five hundred other new hires like me, it was the difference between employment and unemployment. I hit the mark, made the grade, and passed my test. I was now at the home office about to start my training in my new career.

The "Know Your Customer" (KYC) class is designed to teach us how to present a financial idea, overcome the customer's objections and ask for the order (their business) within a week. Coming from a military background since age seventeen, I'd never sold anything in my life, unless you consider my brief time at McDonalds where I was fired for eating the French fries as a teenager. So, how in the world was I going to do this? I had no idea about investments? I thought that a bond was something you paid to get someone out of jail! Besides, this was a sales job, and I did not like pushy salesmen, probably because I'm married to one.

The negative self-talk began in my head as I looked around the room and observed my counterparts. Things like, "You're going to fail, you have no business being here, no one in this room looks like you, etc." kept going through my mind. Everyone else looked nervous, or at least unsure of themselves. I noticed someone who looked distinctively different from the rest of us. He sat tall in his chair. Confidence radiated from his strong smile. We made eye contact, and I felt at ease. "Who is this guy?" I thought. "Why is he here?" Our chairs were aligned in a circular fashion and he was in the center. I thought, "He must be important."

The instructor entered the classroom and introduced herself. She then introduced Mr. Confidence, who was sitting in the middle of the room. His title was Visiting Veteran. He had been with Edward Jones Investments for over 20 years and he was a Level 10 advisor, the highest level. The Visiting Veteran is there to help train, motivate and offer ideas to us junior advisors. They are also there after the class for the junior advisor to call on for advice and support. Each week, hundreds of junior advisors come to St Louis for the KYC class, and then are sent out to the field to build their book of business.

During the initial hiring from year one to four, which is the building phase of your business, junior advisors drop like flies. They don't make the cut. Once again, it reminded me of boot camp. The constant rejection, disappointments, and unkept promises are enough to make the strongest person throw their hands in the air and quit. My husband Steve says it is the toughest career that he knows. The television show Deadliest Catch has been alleged to be one of the hardest jobs in America. Trust me; It can't compare to getting someone to talk about their money, give you their money, and trust you with their money.

Mr. Confidence began sharing his journey with us. He told about his days sitting in that very room feeling the exact same way we felt. He assured us that we would be fine if we worked hard and followed Jones' proven success system. As he continued to speak, he said something on that first day that has been with me throughout my career. He continued to share with us how he got started and how he built a Level 10 business. He said that in the very beginning of his career, he told himself, "There is No Plan B." He went on to say that if he knew there was something else out there that he could be doing, then he would not give this opportunity everything he had to give. So, he would constantly tell himself, "There is No Plan B." "Wow." I thought to myself, "There is No Plan B." I kept saying that to myself over and over again. "There is No Plan B." "There is no Plan B." "There is No Plan B." I have to do this! I must be successful! My family is depending on me! My kids need me to do this! I will not fail!" By the way, this type of talk is called positive self-talk. You should do it daily regarding your life and your business.

Tony Robbins calls them incantations. Incantations are meant to be emotional support or encouragement. Yes, you can offer support and encouragement to yourself. I began to look back over my life. I thought of how I joined the Navy with No Plan B because my step-father had already told me not to return home. I had no choice but to make it work. One of the problems within our society is that too many people have a plan B. We have the attitude, "Oh well, if this doesn't work out for me then I'll go and do something else." So, we don't fully commit ourselves. We must develop a No Plan B attitude. In your marriage, No Plan B. In your job, No Plan B. In your business, No Plan B. Faith was birthed in me that day for this career.

Throughout the last six years, there have been plenty of times when I wanted to quit; plenty of times when I wanted to give up. But I could always hear my visiting veteran say, "Erin, there is No Plan B." Then I would lick my wounds, dust myself off and get back in the fight. Some days my pity party would last a little longer than usual, but eventually, I always got back up. Because of my "No Plan B" attitude, I am now entering into my sixth year as a financial advisor and still going strong. My name is also etched in stone on the Leaders Board at the home office. I was recently appointed as a Field Trainer to new advisors in our area, and I constantly receive job offers from other companies. The answer is always no because as I said, I don't have a Plan B.

So, I have to ask you, is your Plan B the reason you are not giving your dreams everything you've got? Do you have something else you can always fall back on? Are you working your part-time job rather than working on your dream part-time? Is your dream the Plan

B? Do you keep telling yourself, "I will do it one day?" As long as there is a Plan B, we will not work harder. As long as there is a plan B we will not give it all we've got. As long as there is a Plan B we will not fully commit ourselves. There will always be some energy left in the reserve tank, just in case, or for our exit strategy. Steve has given you several chapters on working harder, but I submit to you that you will not work harder with a Plan B in your back pocket. You will only give so much! You know it, and I know it! So, at what point do we stop lying to ourselves?

Now depending on who you speak with, you will find different opinions regarding Plan B. Some say it's wise to have a back-up plan. Speaker Jeff Jones observed, "If you want to succeed, Plan A is the only way." Charlie Day remarked, "Thinking of Plan B muddies up your chances of succeeding at Plan A." Dr. John C. Maxwell mentioned, "Leaders who practice the law of victory believe that anything less than success is unacceptable. And they have no Plan B." Will Smith commented, "There is no reason to have a Plan B because it distracts from Plan A." And when someone says, "Be realistic. You should always have a plan B." Will responds, "Being realistic is the most commonly traveled road to mediocrity."

In the year 1519, Hernan Cortez arrived in the New World with six hundred men and, upon arrival, made history by destroying his ships. "Burn the ships" he told them. This sent a clear message to his men: There is no turning back. There is No Plan B. Two years later he succeeded in his conquest of the Aztec empire. At what point, do we burn the ships like Captain Cortez? I can imagine the look on the men's faces. I'm sure the whispers around the camp were, "He has lost his mind." But that order caused them to dig deeper than they ever would have, had the ships been sitting on the shoreline the entire time. He made the term "do or die" very real to them. So often we say things like, "I'm going to do this thing, I am in it to win it, or I'm here to the end." But when push comes to shove, we look around and you have quit and gone back to your Plan B.

Nobody Cares, Work Harder has given you the tools to go out and seize the moment, realize your dreams, and become all that you were created to be in life and business. It will only work if you eliminate the Plan B from your life. Will you burn your ship? Will you remove your comfort zone suit and jump? Will you give it all you've got? Or, will you settle for your Plan B?

NOBODY CARES... WORK HARDER

TO BOOK STEVE TO SPEAK AT YOUR NEXT EVENT OR TO BUY BOOKS GO TO WWW.STEVEWILMER.COM

Made in the USA
Columbia, SC
12 January 2018